Guidelines for
Management Planning
of Protected Areas

IUCN – The World Conservation Union

Founded in 1948, The World Conservation Union brings together States, government agencies and a diverse range of non-governmental organizations in a unique world partnership: over 1000 members in all, spread across some 140 countries.

As a Union, IUCN seeks to influence, encourage and assist societies throughout the world to conserve the integrity and diversity of nature and to ensure that any use of natural resources is equitable and ecologically sustainable. A central secretariat co-ordinates the IUCN Programme and serves the Union membership, representing their views on the world stage and providing them with the strategies, services, scientific knowledge and technical support they need to achieve their goals. Through its six Commissions, IUCN draws together over 10,000 expert volunteers in project teams and action groups, focusing in particular on species and biodiversity conservation and the management of habitats and natural resources. The Union has helped many countries to prepare National Conservation Strategies, and demonstrates the application of its knowledge through the field projects it supervises. Operations are increasingly decentralized and are carried forward by an expanding network of regional and country offices, located principally in developing countries.

The World Conservation Union builds on the strengths of its members, networks and partners to enhance their capacity and to support global alliances to safeguard natural resources at local, regional and global levels.

Cardiff University

The Department of City and Regional Planning, Cardiff University is pleased to be a partner in the production of this important series of guidelines for protected area planning and management. The Department, through its Environmental Planning Research Unit, is actively involved in protected areas research; runs specialised courses on planning and environmental policy; and has a large Graduate School offering opportunities for persons interested in pursuing research for a PhD or as part of wider career development. If you are interested in learning more about the Department, its research capabilities and courses please write to us at the address given below.

Professor Terry Marsden BAHon., PhD, MRTPI
Head of Department
Department of City and Regional Planning
Cardiff University
Glamorgan Building
King Edward VIIth Avenue
Cardiff, CFl0 3WA, Wales, UK

Tel: + 44 2920 874022
Fax: + 44 2920 874845
E-mail: MarsdenTK@cf.ac.uk
Web site: www.cf.ac.uk

Guidelines for Management Planning of Protected Areas

Lee Thomas and Julie Middleton

Adrian Phillips, Series Editor

World Commission on Protected Areas (WCPA)

Best Practice Protected Area Guidelines Series No. 10

IUCN – The World Conservation Union
2003

This publication has been made possible by funding from Cardiff University, IUCN and the World Bank/GEF.

Published by: IUCN, Gland, Switzerland, and Cambridge, UK

Copyright: © 2003 International Union for Conservation of Nature and Natural Resources

Citation: Thomas, Lee and Middleton, Julie, (2003). *Guidelines for Management Planning of Protected Areas*. IUCN Gland, Switzerland and Cambridge, UK. ix + 79pp.

ISBN: 2-8317-0673-4

Cover design: IUCN Publications Services Unit

Cover photos: Front: Training ©*Jim Thorsell*

Back: Aerial view of the St Lucia estuary mouth, with the mouth of the Mfolozi estuary in the distance © *R. de la Harpe*; Ranger and hikers, Mt Cook, New Zealand ©*Jim Thorsell* and the St Katherine area, Egypt ©*Jim Thorsell*

Layout by: IUCN Publications Services Unit

Produced by: IUCN Publications Services Unit

Printed by: Thanet Press Limited, UK

Available from: IUCN Publications Services Unit
219c Huntingdon Road, Cambridge CB3 0DL,
United Kingdom
Tel: +44 1223 277894
Fax: +44 1223 277175
E-mail: info@iucn.org
www.iucn.org/bookstore
A catalogue of IUCN publications is also available

Table of Contents

Foreword   vii
Acknowledgements   viii
About the authors   ix

1. Introduction   1

2. Definitions and background   3
   2.1   Protected areas   3
   2.2   Management planning   4
   2.3   Budget   5
   2.4   Time requirements   6
   2.5   Management by objectives   6
   2.6   Management Plan   6
   2.7   Other plans associated with the Management Plan   7
   2.8   Why plan?   9
   2.9   Legislative, statutory or other requirements   9
   2.10 The benefits of management planning   10
   2.11 Implementation of national or regional policies and corporate
         strategies   12

**3. Requirements for successful preparation and implementation
of Management Plans**   15
   3.1   Introduction – what works   15
   3.2   The process used in plan preparation   15
   3.3   The presentation, style and content of the Management Plan   17
   3.4   The context within which the plan must operate   18
   3.5   Resources, commitment and capacity   19
   3.6   Problems encountered in planning and implementation   21
   3.7   Abbreviated forms of planning   22

4. The management planning process   23
   4.1   Overview of the process   23
   4.2   Preparing a Management Plan   25
         Step 1. Pre-planning phase   25
         Step 2. Data collection, background research and initial fieldwork 26
         Step 3. Evaluating the information   31
         Step 4. Identifying constraints, opportunities and threats   32
         Step 5. Developing management vision and objectives   33

Step 6. Identifying and evaluating options including zoning 38

Step 7. Integration into a draft plan 42

Step 8. Public consultation, including public exhibition of the draft plan 47

Step 9. Revision of draft and production of final plan 49

Step 10. Approval of plan 49

Step 11. Implementation of the Management Plan 49

Step 12. Monitoring and review 51

Step 13. Decision to review and update the Management Plan 53

5. Involving people 55

5.1 Why involve people 55

5.2 Whom to involve 56

5.3 Types of involvement 57

5.4 Consultation 58

5.5 Methods 59

5.6 Towards community based planning 61

6. The international dimension to management planning 65

6.1 The management of World Heritage sites 65

6.2 Ramsar Sites 66

6.3 UNESCO Biosphere Reserves 67

6.4 Protected areas subject to international or regional agreements 67

6.5 Transboundary arrangements 67

7. Abbreviated planning approaches 69

Annex: Roles, responsibilities and skills 71

The planning team 71

The project manager, the planner and the author 72

References 75

Foreword

Management Planning is an essential step towards ensuring the proper management of protected areas. This is particularly so as we move forward to the 21st century and face increasing complexities in the management of our parks and reserves. The essential steps of good management planning embracing current best practice are not always understood by park agencies or planning practitioners. So I am pleased to see the publication of these Guidelines, which have been compiled by two very experienced planners.

In past years, management planning was typically undertaken by a group of planning experts who were instructed by their organisation to research the relevant information, interpret it and devise the best possible plan based on their professional experience. Indeed some planners may never have visited the site. Today, as we move into increasingly complex planning environments, with higher levels of tourism and protected area resource use, it is not possible to continue in this way. Critical to the planning of protected areas is the widest possible consultation with stakeholders and the development of objectives that can be agreed and adhered to by all who have an interest in the use and ongoing survival of the area concerned. So I am pleased to see that the consultative phase, particularly with local communities, features strongly in these Guidelines.

It needs to be recognised that the preparation of the plans can be expensive and time consuming. While short cuts can be taken, this will be to the detriment of the protected area. Those organisations with responsibility for management are urged to make the strongest possible commitment to planning so as to avoid the long-term perils of management which lacks a strategic direction.

In the past, emphasis in management planning has been almost exclusively directed towards biological, ecological, physical and cultural aspects. As these Guidelines make clear we need to go beyond this. This represents the starting point for the work of the planners who need to reach out and take into account as never before the myriad of use patterns, the often complex organisational arrangements, the range of economic services generated, the financial aspects and the "benefits beyond boundaries" to those outside the park borders.

It is very pleasing that these Guidelines comprehensively move management planning into the new millennium. I am pleased to offer my strong endorsement of them.

Kenton Miller
Chair – World Commission on Protected Areas

Acknowledgements

IUCN, Cardiff University and the authors are indebted to Ms Kathy Mackinnon and the World Bank/GEF for their support in enabling these guidelines to be produced.

The authors also wish to acknowledge the prior work of the many authors and organisations cited in these guidelines. They have contributed to the collective protected areas management planning wisdom which has been developed further here. The long list of references testifies to the breadth and depth of these contributions upon which this publication has been able to draw.

The work of those who reviewed the draft text and provided valuable comments is also gratefully acknowledged.

About the authors

Lee Thomas is one of two Deputy Chairs of the IUCN World Commission on Protected Areas. He holds a Bachelor Degree in Technology and a Masters in Business Administration and is a consultant specialising in Protected Area Management. Between 1987 and 2002 he worked for Parks Australia in a senior position with responsibilities for a wide range of functions including management, planning and policy development for both terrestrial and marine protected areas.

Julie Middleton has a Bachelor of Science Degree in Ecological Sciences, a Masters in Forestry Resource Management and a Masters in Environment and Development. She spent six years with the National Trust for Scotland, preparing Management Plans for the many protected areas, landscapes and cultural sites in its care. She is currently employed in South Africa by a consultancy firm specialising in providing advice on policy, economics and management to the public sector.

1. Introduction

What is a Management Plan for a protected area? Why is one needed?

In simple terms, a Management Plan is a document which sets out the management approach and goals, together with a framework for decision making, to apply in the protected area over a given period of time. Plans may be more or less prescriptive, depending upon the purpose for which they are to be used and the legal requirements to be met. The process of planning, the management objectives for the plan and the standards to apply will usually be established in legislation or otherwise set down for protected area planners.

Management Plans should be succinct documents that identify the key features or values of the protected area, clearly establish the management objectives to be met and indicate the actions to be implemented. They also need to be flexible enough to cater for unforeseen events which might arise during the currency of the plan. Related documents to the Management Plan may include more detailed zoning, visitor and business plans to guide its implementation. However the Management Plan is the prime document from which other plans flow, and it should normally take precedence if there is doubt or conflict.

The process of developing a Management Plan may be more or less complex depending upon the objectives of the protected area, the risks or threats to these objectives, the number of competing interests, the level of stakeholder[1] involvement and the issues arising from outside the protected area. Whether the plan is simple or complex, sound planning principles should be applied to guide the planning process and ensure that the completed Management Plan is a thorough and useful document. These Guidelines, based on global best practice drawn from many areas around the world, represent a working framework for protected area planners to consider and adapt to their needs and circumstances.

References to management planning can also be found in most of the previous publications in the IUCN/Cardiff Best Practice series. In particular:

- Number 1: *National System Planning for Protected Areas* – especially page 28;
- Number 3: *Guidelines for Marine Protected Areas* – especially pages 79–87;
- Number 5: *Financing Protected Areas: Guidelines for Protected Area Managers* – especially page 26;
- Number 6: *Evaluating Effectiveness: A Framework for Assessing the Management of Protected Areas* – especially pages 11–12;
- Number 7: *Transboundary Protected Areas for Peace and Co-operation* – especially pages 27–29;
- Number 8: *Sustainable Tourism in Protected Areas* – especially pages 41–59; and

---

[1] 'Stakeholder' is used here to mean someone who is directly affected by the outcome of the planning process.

1

■ Number 9: *Management Guidelines for IUCN Category V Protected Areas: Protected Landscapes/Seascapes* – especially pages 95–102 and 113–117.

This publication builds on and consolidates the experience and advice contained in these earlier publications in the same series, as well as in other sources (see References). In accordance with the practice used in several of the Best Practice series, specific guidance is identified thus in the text: **Guidelines**.

The structure of the publication is as follows:

■ Chapter 2 introduces basic concepts and definitions

■ Chapter 3 explains the requirements for successful management planning

■ Chapter 4 describes the management planning process

■ Chapter 5 sets out what needs to be done to involve people in management planning

■ Chapter 6 deals with the international dimension to management planning

■ Chapter 7 sets out an abbreviated management planning system where it is not possible to adopt the full process.

The Annex discusses the roles and responsibilities of people involved in the management planning process.

These management planning guidelines have generally been written in the context of management being exercised by a central, provincial or local government body. However it is recognised that the management responsibility for an increasing number of protected areas lies with other kinds of organisations. Indeed, in many countries non-governmental organisations, private owners, community groups, indigenous peoples and others are increasingly involved in setting up and managing protected areas. In particular, many communities have over long periods of time managed what are in effect protected areas, though often their efforts have gone unrecognised by the authorities. References to the "protected area agency" or "protected area authority" should therefore be interpreted widely. Irrespective of the kind of managing body in place, the Guidelines offered here are intended to apply to all protected areas.

Chapter 5, which presents the involvement of the community and stakeholders in the planning process, is a particularly important part of these Guidelines. The opportunity for involvement underpins the success of the planning effort. Just as competent planners are important to the outcome, so is an open and well conducted process for involving those who will ultimately be impacted by the Management Plan. Close attention should be paid to this chapter in the overall management planning process.

2. Definitions and background

2.1 Protected areas

IUCN defines a protected area as:

"An area of land and/or sea especially dedicated to the protection of biological diversity, and of natural and associated cultural resources, and managed through legal or other effective means" (IUCN 1994).

Protected areas can be categorised into six types, according to their management objectives:

Category I Protected area managed mainly for science or wilderness protection (I(a) Strict Nature Reserves, and I(b) Wilderness Areas).

Category II Protected area managed mainly for ecosystem protection and recreation (National Park).

Category III Protected area managed mainly for conservation of specific natural features (Natural Monument).

Category IV Protected area managed mainly for conservation through management intervention.

Category V Protected area managed mainly for landscape/seascape conservation and recreation (Protected Landscape/Seascape).

Category VI Protected area managed mainly for the sustainable use of natural ecosystems (Managed Resource Protected Area).[1]

While each of the protected area categories has a different range of management objectives, all the categories should have one feature in common: a properly thought through Management Plan process to ensure that the optimum outcomes are achieved.

In addition to conserving biological and cultural diversity, it is now widely recognised that many protected areas also have important social and economic functions. These include protecting watersheds, soil and coastlines, providing natural products for use on a sustainable basis, and supporting tourism and recreation. Many protected areas are also home to communities of people with traditional cultures and knowledge: these assets also need protection. Since most protected areas have multiple objectives, there is a need to consider a wide array of social preferences and values (both for present and future generations), institutional structures and barriers, philosophical outlooks, forms of knowledge and conflicting opinions of what is important. Because all these various considerations have to be taken into account, the task of preparing Management Plans for protected areas can be challenging, yet it is essential for the well being of the natural and cultural resources being managed.

---

[1] For a fuller explanation, see *Guidelines for Protected Area Management Categories*, IUCN (1994).

This wider, more inclusive approach to protected area management has emerged in recent years. The trend has been captured in the following new "paradigm" for protected areas (Table 1).

Table 1 A new paradigm for protected areas

Topic	As it was: protected areas were …	As it is becoming: protected areas are …
Objectives	■ Set aside for conservation ■ Established mainly for spectacular wildlife and scenic protection ■ Managed mainly for visitors and tourists ■ Valued as wilderness ■ About protection	■ Run also with social and economic objectives ■ Often set up for scientific, economic and cultural reasons ■ Managed with local people more in mind ■ Valued for the cultural importance of so-called "wilderness" ■ Also about restoration and rehabilitation
Governance	Run by central government	Run by many partners and involve an array of stakeholders
Local people	■ Planned and managed against people ■ Managed without regard to local opinions	■ Run with, for, and in some cases by local people ■ Managed to meet the needs of local people
Wider context	■ Developed separately ■ Managed as 'islands'	■ Planned as part of national, regional and international systems ■ Developed as 'networks' (strictly protected areas, buffered and linked by green corridors)
Perceptions	■ Viewed primarily as a national asset ■ Viewed only as a national concern	■ Viewed also as a community asset ■ Viewed also as an international concern
Management techniques	■ Managed reactively within a short timescale ■ Managed in a technocratic way	■ Managed adaptively in a long term perspective ■ Managed with political considerations
Finance	Paid for by taxpayer	Paid for from many sources
Management skills	■ Managed by scientists and natural resource experts ■ Expert led	■ Managed by multi-skilled individuals ■ Drawing on local knowledge

Source: Phillips [in print].

2.2 Management planning

There are many definitions of management planning. Fundamentally, it is a subset of the more general discipline of planning. It has been applied to protected areas in some parts of the developed world since the middle of the 20th century and is now carried out across the globe – but with varying degrees of success. It is a 'tool' to guide managers and other interested parties on how an area should be managed, today and in the future. Its effectiveness depends on a number of factors which will be outlined in more detail in later chapters.

As a management tool, planning helps protected area managers to define and then achieve the mandate of the protected area under their care. As will be seen in the *Guidelines* in Box 1, management planning is **a process – not an event**. Management planning does not end with the production of the plan, important as this might be. Good practice requires that ongoing monitoring take place to test the effectiveness of the plan. Lessons learnt from monitoring should be used to review the appropriateness of management purposes and policies. This feedback loop may thus lead to adjustments to the original plan to keep it on the right track; or the lessons learnt can be used to develop the next version of the plan. The latter will be the case where plans are legislative documents and not easily amended during their term of currency.

Since the Management Plan is a product of a process of management planning, much more is required than a 'manual' on how to prepare a plan. Resources, skills and organisational systems are needed to ensure success in management planning. These issues are outlined in more detail in later Chapters.

Box 1. *Guidelines* on management planning

Successful management planning will be characterised by these features:

- It is a **process**, not an **event** i.e. it does not end with the production of a plan, but continues through its implementation and beyond.

- It is concerned with the **future**: it identifies concerns and future alternative courses of action, and examines the evolving chains of causes and effects likely to result from current decisions.

- It provides a **mechanism** for thinking about threats and opportunities and other difficult issues, **solving problems** and **promoting discussion** between involved parties.

- It is **systematic:** most planning exercises work through a pre-determined sequence of steps that give structure to the process and encourage a logical approach. A systematic approach helps to ensure that decisions are based on knowledge and analysis of the subject and its context, and helps others to understand the rationale for proposed actions.

- It also involves **value judgements.** Management planning can be thought of as a "process which embraces the identification of what a [protected area] is and what it **should** become and how to maintain or attain that desired condition in the face of changing internal and external conditions"(Lipscombe 1987). The use of the word 'should' implies that value judgements help determine what 'should be', as well as 'what is'. Planning for protected areas is thus centred not only on analysis of the objective condition of the natural resource, but also on people and their opinions.

- It takes a **'holistic'** view. The planning process can, if carried out openly and inclusively, take into consideration a very wide range of issues, views and opinions. When applied to a particular area, it should be able to include all processes and issues arising within it, as well as those arising outside its boundaries. How integrated or 'holistic' the process is will depend, however, on how the process is carried out, who is involved and how the final decisions are made.

- It is a **continuous** process; it is never static; it must adjust to changing conditions and goals.

2.3 Budget

Before embarking on a Management Plan, there needs to be a clear idea of the costs and resources available. This is particularly the case where there are to be resource and user surveys, public consultation and possibly the engagement of consultants. A realistic appraisal needs to be made to ensure all costs associated with the plan can be fully met, bearing in mind that the planning may take some years to complete.

Where resources are not available, the manager must decide whether the process should be deferred until a later time. Alternatively there is the option of an abbreviated planning process as set out in Chapter 7.

Importantly there also needs to be recognition of costs to implement the plan so that a measure of consistency exists between what is being planned and what can realistically be expected to be implemented.

2.4 Time requirements

The time needed to prepare a Management Plan, for even a small site, is rarely less than 12 months. Where extensive consultation is required or complex issues must be addressed, it may be considerably more. The processes, which involve seeking public comment, drafting of the document and consultation, are time consuming. As with budgetary requirements, an estimate of time to complete the task should be made at the outset and allowed for.

2.5 Management by objectives

In the broader field of management science, the style of management brought about by management planning is known as 'management by objectives'. Management by objectives is proactive rather than reactive. It is also 'results-oriented', emphasising accomplishments and outcomes. It is an approach that encourages active management by the organisation and is adopted by most well regarded protected area agencies.

Four distinct steps have been identified within this type of management and decision-making:

1. formulation of clear, concise statements or objectives;

2. development of realistic action plans for their attainment (including an analysis of threats to attaining the objectives);

3. systematic monitoring and measuring of performance and achievement; and

4. taking corrective actions necessary to achieve planned results.

These steps correspond to those recommended in the management planning process, which are identified later in Chapter 4.

2.6 Management Plan

The Management Plan is a product of the planning process, documenting the management approach, the decisions made, the basis for these, and the guidance for future management.

The Management Plan should cover the entire protected area. It should contain information on what is to be achieved by management and the rationale behind the management decisions made. Box 2 contains some useful definitions of a Management Plan.

Box 2.   Management Plans

A Management Plan has been variously defined as::

1. "a written, circulated and approved document which describes the site or area and the problems and opportunities for management of its nature conservation, land form or landscape features, enabling objectives based on this information to be met through relevant work over a stated period of time" (Eurosite 1999).

2. "the guide by which Parks Canada manages the resources and uses of a national park. It contains the management objectives and the means and strategies for achieving them. The plan is not an end in itself; rather it constitutes a framework within which subsequent management, implementation and planning will take place" (Parks Canada 1978).

3. "a document that guides and controls the management of a protected area. It details the resources, uses, facilities and personnel needed to manage the area in the future. It is a working document that presents a program for the coming 5–10 years" (Ndosi 1992).

4. "a document that guides and controls the management of protected area resources, the uses of the area and the development of facilities needed to support that management and use. Thus a Management Plan is a working document to guide and facilitate all development activities and all management activities to be implemented in an area" (Thorsell 1995).

5. "a document that sets forth the basic and development philosophy of the park and provides strategies for solving problems and achieving identified management objectives over a ten-year period. Based on these strategies, programs, actions and support facilities necessary for efficient park operations, visitor use and human benefit are identified. Throughout the planning effort, the park is considered in a regional context that influences and is influenced by it" (Young and Young 1993).

2.7   Other plans associated with the Management Plan

The Management Plan is usually accompanied by a number of other plans or related documents, which derive from, or support it. Terminology varies from country to country and there may be some overlap between the following terms:

- **Operational plans** (often called work plans, action plans or implementation plans). These may be produced to present detailed information on how/when specific management actions will be carried out. Such plans are particularly necessary for large and/or complex protected areas, though most sites should prepare them. Typically, operational plans will have a shorter time scale than the Management Plan, for example as annual work plans.

- **Corporate plans** are business plans for the protected area agency. These will explain how the agency operates, set out its objectives and priorities, and provide a means to measure its performance in relation to these. Corporate plans should clearly flow – and be seen to flow – from Management Plans (see IUCN Category V Guidelines).

- **Business plans** are plans to help the protected area be more financially self-sufficient. These examine the "customer base", goods and services, marketing and implementation strategy for the protected area. (For a fuller explanation of the business plan concept, and of the related financial plan, see IUCN 2000a).

- **Zoning plans.** These are produced when different areas or 'zones' of a protected area are to be managed in different ways. They identify the boundaries of the zones and contain detail on how each of the zones is to be managed.[2] Zoning plans provide additional definition and help implement the Management Plan, and are sometimes a part of it.

- **Sectoral plans** may also be required for different management activities, for example interpretation, visitor management and species protection. These are more detailed than the Management Plan, but lead from it – taking their direction from the overall management objectives for the area provided by the Management Plan.

- **Development plans** may be required to guide investment and works affecting a part of the area – for example for particular infrastructure like a visitor centre.

- **Site management plans.** Within larger protected areas, these may be produced for sites within the area that require intensive management, for example, around a major visitor attraction.

- **Conservation plans.** While in general this could mean any plan that provides guidance on how to conserve a site, the term is now used mainly in cultural heritage conservation. Thus a conservation plan is usually a plan for a heritage building or site, where an owner, manager or developer is planning action of some kind (such as restoration, conservation, or installation of a modern structure into older fabric). The conservation plan will explain why the site is significant and how its cultural significance can best be retained and protected. Evaluation and understanding of the significance of the site is at the heart of a conservation plan. This approach has been useful in developing Management Plans for 'mixed sites' where natural and cultural heritage are found together and where an integrated approach is required.

- **Master plans.** Early articles on park planning in the US or Canada in the 1970s often referred to 'Master Plans'. These were considered to be guides for park protection, management, interpretation and development. However, in an early issue of IUCN's *PARKS* magazine (1977), Eidsvik argued that 'master plan' implied an unrealistic degree of permanence within the document; he thought the term 'Management Plan' should be used instead. This was supported by MacKinnon *et al.* (1986) in their publication on the management of protected areas in the tropics. In fact, 'master plan' has been little used since the 1970s, and has now been superseded by Management Plans, corporate and strategic plans.

With all these kinds of plans, one may ask what is required within the Management Plan itself ? – and indeed whether one Management Plan will 'do' or whether other types of plan are necessary?

The level of operational detail to include in a Management Plan is a decision for each agency to determine. How detailed the plan should be in terms of its operational content will most probably depend on whether there are other systems (e.g. for work planning) set up within the organisation or whether the Management Plan is expected to provide the detailed day-to-day guidance for the manager. There will be pros and cons to any approach taken, but whether the information is presented in the Management Plan or in separate operational or other plans, it is important that strategic and operational elements

---

[2] More detail on zoning and zoning plans is given in section 4.2, Step 6.

are present in some form and are clearly linked. If the strategic directions are missing or poorly developed, the plan will lack coherence: if the operational element is missing, the objectives defined within the rest of the Management Plan will never be achieved. (Chapter 4 will contain a further discussion of how much detail and operational information should be included in a Management Plan).

2.8 Why plan?

Frequently much time and effort is put into management planning for protected areas but the plans are not used – or are unusable[3]. Even in these circumstances there is general agreement about the desirability of such plans; their preparation is supported by most conservation agencies and IUCN wishes to see plans in place for all protected areas (IUCN/Caracas Action Plan 1992). Management Plans bring many benefits to protected areas and to the organisations or individuals charged with their management – and, without them, serious problems can ensue:

'If there is no general Management Plan, preservation, development and use activities in a park will occur in a haphazard basis, often in response to political pressures with little consideration as to the implications for the future. The result is likely to be lost opportunities and irreversible damage to park resources and values' (Young and Young 1993).

2.9 Legislative, statutory or other requirements

In some countries, managers of protected areas are obliged to prepare Management Plans as a requirement of legislation. This is the case, for example, for national parks in Australia (*Environmental Protection and Biodiversity Conservation Act 1999*) and England and Wales (*Environment Act 1995*). Such legislation provides the managing organisations with a statutory instruction to prepare plans (often, the legislation or statutory advice dictates the form and contents of the plan and the process to be followed in its preparation).

Management Plans may be required to meet other legislative requirements. Thus in many jurisdictions, Management Plans have the status of legal documents and provide the protected area managers with the mandate to manage parks and expend public monies. Failure to manage a protected area in accordance with the plan may give rise to an offence and legal action. A legal basis is essential for effective compliance and enforcement action by managers.

Legislation of this kind may also forbid certain actions except where provided for under the Management Plan: for example, they may forbid the import of exotic plant materials into a national park unless this is specifically provided for under the plan. Thus the requirements of the legislation need to be carefully examined to ensure that all relevant provisions are covered in the plan.

Management Plans are normally required for natural sites that are being considered for inclusion on the World Heritage List. The UNESCO Operational Guidelines (see also Chapter 6) specify the exact nature of this requirement:

"Sites should have a Management Plan. When a site does not have a Management Plan at the time when it is nominated for the consideration of the World Heritage

---

[3] Chapter 3 of these Guidelines will identify what contributes to a successful Management Plan, and conversely, what factors lead to a less than useful plan.

Committee, the State Party concerned should indicate when such a plan will become available and how it proposes to mobilise the resources required for preparation and implementation of the plan. The State Party should also provide other documents (e.g. operational plans) which will guide the management of the site until such time when a Management Plan is finalised" (UNESCO 1999).

Also, many donors (and especially multilateral and bilateral donors) that support protected area projects require that a Management Plan be produced as part of the funding agreement. They see this as central to the effective management of the area, encouraging the wise use of the funds and introducing a framework of accountability for the project.

2.10 The benefits of management planning

Apart from meeting legislative requirements, the most compelling reason for producing Management Plans is to provide benefits to the protected area and those who rely upon its good management. A good management planning process which has the support of staff and local people, provides the following benefits:

Improved management of the protected area

The primary product of management planning should be more **effective management** of the protected area. Management planning encourages more effective management by:

1. ensuring that management decisions are based on a clear **understanding** of the protected area, its purpose, and the important resources and values associated with it.

2. providing **guidance for managers** in the form of a framework for day-to-day operations and long-term management. A Management Plan should provide the manager with a long-term vision for the protected area, as well as guidance on how to direct the management of the protected area towards this vision. It should assist in day-to-day decisions about complex problems, by clarifying management objectives and prioritising them. This should resolve conflicts, address bad risks, remove ambiguity on how the area is to be managed and explain how the decisions were arrived at.

3. providing **continuity** of management. Having an agreed Management Plan in place provides a useful briefing document for new staff and helps them to maintain the direction and momentum of management. This is particularly important for small or voluntary organisations where there is high staff turnover, and management may be carried out by a succession of staff and volunteers.

4. by helping to identify and define management '**effectiveness**'. If the management objectives within a Management Plan are well written, specific and can be measured, they can be used as a basis for determining whether management of the protected area is effective or whether changes in management (or indeed in the plan) are required. (A fuller discussion of this topic is to be found in Best Practice Guidelines No. 6, Hockings *et al.*, 2000).

Improved use of financial and staff resources

Management planning can help make sensible use of resources. For example:

1. Management Plans (and any associated operational, corporate and business plans) identify, describe and prioritise the management actions required to achieve the objectives for the protected area. This list of tasks helps managers to allocate the staff, funding and materials required. Many organisations also link their annual work plans for protected areas to annual budgets, ensuring more efficient financial planning and control.

2. Management Plans may also highlight where additional resources are required. In this way a plan can act as a fundraising tool, although if an organisation cannot meet the total resources required to implement the plan, it would be better to modify it, than allow it to become a mere 'wish list'.

Increased accountability

Management planning can provide a mechanism for increasing the accountability of:

1. **the protected area manager(s)**. The manager should be mandated to work within the Management Plan, which can then be used to identify targets to reach and performance standards to attain. The plan can also be used by managers to draw up work plans for staff, assign duties, and monitor and assess performance. It also discourages a manager from 'acting on whim'.

2. **the managing organisations/agencies**. A plan can act as a sort of public contract between the manager, local communities and visitors on how the protected area will be managed and protected in future. Thus the Management Plan can provide a way by which the public can examine management decisions and monitor delivery against targets.

Improved communication

The management planning process can provide a useful link between the protected area manager and those with an interest in the area, its management and future. It does this by:

1. identifying **key audiences** with whom the manager needs to communicate, and clarifying the messages to be communicated.

2. providing a means of **communication with the public**, to explain policies and proposals. In particular the Management Plan (and the planning process) can be used to gain the co-operation of the public and non-governmental organisations. This function should influence the style and presentation of the plan as it will need to be easily understood by non-specialists. A Management Plan should function as an interpretative document, being designed as much for the public as for the manager. Planning should be conducted to encourage public interest and support for the plan.

3. promoting and publicising the protected area to a wide range of **stakeholders**.

As summarised by the US National Park Service:

"Through public involvement [in the management planning process] the National Park Service will share information about the planning process, issues and proposed management actions; learn about the values placed by other people and groups on the same resources and visitor experiences; and build support among local publics, visitors, Congress and others for implementing the plan" (USNPS 1998).

Fig. 1   Typical planning hierarchy

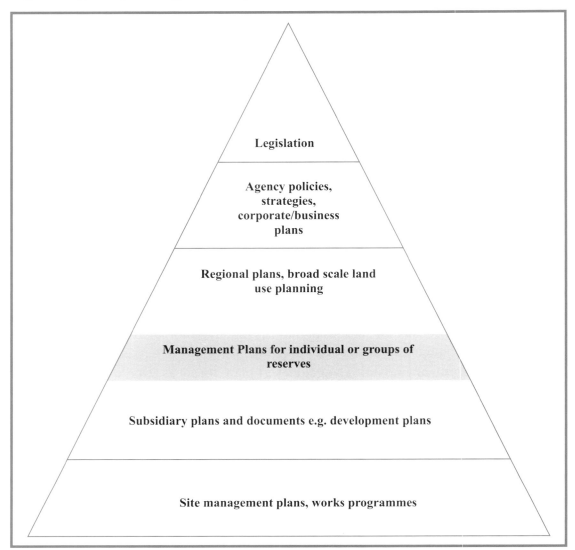

Source: Adapted from Best Practice in Protected Area Management ANZECC Working Group May 2000.

2.11   Implementation of national or regional policies and corporate strategies

Management planning often involves the interpretation and expression of broader policies at the local level: that is, the local delivery of broader strategy. Plans should also be written to:

1. ensure that international obligations are met, for example those under the World Heritage or Ramsar (wetlands) Conventions, or under regional agreements like the EU's Birds and Habitats Directives (see also Chapter 6);

2. implement at the site level relevant recommendations from any national systems plan for protected areas (see Davey, 1998);

3. implement national conservation and environmental directives/initiatives (for example, national species and habitat action plans in the UK are delivered through Management Plans for sites within the UK); and

4. ensure that the management objectives for protected areas reflect corporate policies of the managing organisation (for example, financial management responsibilities).

Thus management planning can and must fulfil many different purposes. These will vary for different protected areas and will depend on the purpose of the protected area and the policies of the managing organisation. The plan may also serve different purposes for different users. It is therefore desirable that the authors(s) of a Management Plan make sure that they identify what is required of the plan before they start the planning process.

3. Requirements for successful preparation and implementation of Management Plans

3.1 Introduction – what works

The previous chapter lists the many benefits a Management Plan can bring to a protected area and its management: and indeed planners, managers and donors are all agreed on the value of management planning. Yet relatively few protected area Management Plans can be considered successful:

> *"By far the most common situation is that [general management and development] plans tend to gather dust or at best receive minimal implementation, despite the tremendous national (and frequently international) technical co-operation efforts which go into their preparation"* (Budowski and MacFarland 1982)

This chapter deals with how such problems can be overcome, and what needs to be done to ensure a successful Management Plan that is useful, practical and can be implemented. The factors that determine whether this is the case come under four main headings:

1. The process used during plan preparation (section 3.2);

2. The presentation, style and content of the resulting plan (section 3.3);

3. The context within which the plan must operate (section 3.4); and

4. The resources, commitment and capacity to implement the plan (section 3.5).

Such factors will affect whether the benefits of Management Plans, as outlined in Chapter 2, are realised.

3.2 The process used in plan preparation

This should be **'participatory'**, involving the people affected by management of the protected area. Participation should take place as early in the process as possible and continue throughout. Two audiences are involved: an external one (local people, visitors and other stakeholders), and an internal one (the staff who will be charged with the plan's implementation). In both cases, the plan is much more likely to be implemented if the affected audiences are involved in its development and have a sense of 'shared ownership'.

It is increasingly the practice to involve local communities and other stakeholders in protected area planning and management. In many countries, Management Boards, co-management structures and other participatory mechanisms are being created to facilitate this. The members of these bodies need access to information about the protected area, including copies of draft and final Management Plans – as indeed will many different groups among the concerned public. There will be a need – even a demand – for consultation over draft plans. Where the Internet is widely used (such as Australia, New Zealand, USA and Canada), this can be used to provide more dispersed user and visitor groups with access to information and as a means of consultation.

In certain cases it may be desirable to make the Management Plan available to local communities in their own language where this differs from the official language. While the cost of this needs to be taken into account, there may be significant advantages in doing so in situations where local people would otherwise have difficulty with understanding the plan and the consultation process.

Chapter 5 discusses the involvement of the local community and other stakeholders in the planning process in more detail. Doing this can significantly increase the degree of local ownership of the process and its product.

With both external and internal audiences, the preparatory process should also:

- be clear and logical, beginning with the identification of management objectives;

- focus on well-defined issues concerning the protection of the important natural and cultural resources of the protected area;

- develop specific actions or alternative options in response to these issues and identify who will be responsible for implementing these actions; and

- identify a clear approach to implementation, including the resources required.

In addition, park staff must be empowered to make sufficient and important contributions to the preparation of a Management Plan, if they are to feel ownership of it and be motivated to implement it. Staff should never be simply presented with plans for implementation. **Guidelines** for building ownership of a Management Plan among staff are provided in Box 3.

Box 3. *Guidelines* for improving 'sense of ownership' of a plan among protected area staff

1. Secure a strong public commitment to the importance of Management Plans by senior personnel, Members of the Board of Management, local government, Ministry officials etc.

2. Ensure that there are real and visible linkages between planning recommendations and budgetary allocations within the organisation.

3. Hold park level meetings to inform staff about the Management Plan at the outset of its preparation, and identify how staff can influence the plan's content and the planning process.

4. Involve staff at key stages in the formulation of the plan, for example by including staff or a staff representative in workshops, and circulating the draft plan to the Worker's Council/ Staff Committee for discussion and comment.

5. Entrust individual members of staff with initiating and scheduling items identified for implementation in the Management Plan.

6. Make copies available to staff of work plans for their reference.

7. Link the Management Plan to annual performance assessments.

3.3 The presentation, style and content of the Management Plan

The presentation, style and content of the completed Management Plan can have a great influence on whether it is well received and understood by users, including the public, and whether it effectively communicates the values of the protected area and the proposed actions contained in the plan. These features will also affect its implementation and the extent of public support for park management.

Box 4 contains **Guidelines** for a 'good' Management Plan. This list represents a sound checklist to use and aspire to.

Box 4. *Guidelines* for a good Management Plan

A Management Plan should be:

1. **Clear and accessible**: easy to read, jargon free and well presented.
2. **Concise and comprehensive**: no longer than is absolutely necessary, but with enough information to fulfil its functions.
3. **Accurate and objective**: without major errors or statements likely to date and with the criteria for all judgements clearly explained.
4. **Systematic and logical**: With management policies derived from an assessment of the site and with a clear rationale given for all proposals.
5. **Acceptable and motivating** to all those with interests in and emotional attachment to the site.
6. **Precise and practical**: with clear objectives, realistic methods for achieving them, resulting in desired outcomes which can be monitored.
7. **Focused and effective**: fulfilling its purpose as a tool for site management, meeting the needs of its users and satisfying any legal or other obligations.

Source: Clarke and Mount (1998).

In addition to the advice in Box 4, a Management Plan should also aim at balancing:

- precision with flexibility;
- comprehensiveness with simplicity; and
- management orientation with ease of understanding by the public.

Flexibility

Logically a Management Plan should be sufficiently flexible to allow for change through its working life. Flexibility is required to ensure that management can adapt to changed situations. As a plan is implemented over its timeframe, managers must be able to learn from experience and to modify their practices accordingly. This is especially important when managing natural areas, where an adaptive management approach is essential.

However, the degree of flexibility available to protected area managers must be tempered by the legislative controls under which a Management Plan is prepared. For example where a Management Plan has been approved by Parliament, as in Australia, it may be possible to vary it with the approval only of the relevant Minister and then only after a period of public comment. In such cases, it may be more appropriate to wait until the plan is formally reviewed and include any necessary changes in the new version.

Alternatively some flexibility can be built in, as long as the decision criteria for choosing between alternatives are clearly set out.

Simplicity

The following quotation emphasises the importance of keeping a plan clear and simple:

"The simpler the plan the easier it will be to develop and implement. It will take less time to prepare, will cost less, will be more flexible to change, will be easier to read and understand and will require fewer staff with lower levels of training – which is especially important in a developing country. Detail and complexity will evolve naturally as the plan is regularly updated and as increased support becomes available" (MacKinnon *et al.*, 1986).

Note also that modest management planning efforts are likely to be more cost effective than more elaborate ones, thus freeing funds and resources for other purposes.

Management oriented

The main focus of a Management Plan should be the clear explanation of the vision, the management objectives needed to realise this and the strategies/actions required to implement them. Many Management Plans lose their impact and clarity because of an over-emphasis on descriptive information about the site. The quest for detailed descriptive information can also significantly delay the production of a plan.

If authors find that the 'management focus' is being diluted by a requirement that the plan perform other interpretive or public relations functions, or if the desire to keep it concise means that it will not effectively fulfil these other functions, then these requirements should be addressed in some other way. For example, separate resource descriptions, policy documents, press releases on management activity or information documents could be produced.

Easily understood

The first point in Box 4 emphasises that Management Plans should be clear and accessible, free of jargon, easy to read and well presented. Given that Management Plans often have a wide and varied audience, this can be difficult to achieve. Therefore, great care and attention must be given to the 'writing' style of a Management Plan. This is often a skill that requires training and practice – a fact that should not be forgotten when staff with little or no experience of management planning are expected to contribute to or take on this very important responsibility.

3.4 The context within which the plan must operate

Regional integration

Management Plans must be prepared and implemented within the context of the lands, issues and peoples surrounding protected areas. Protected area managers need to look beyond their immediate boundaries in planning their areas, e.g. when planning buffer zones and compatible uses, and designing educational, interpretive and public involvement programmes. Regional integration becomes particularly important when others are responsible for administering the area beyond the protected area boundary.

This is a common feature in countries where the national government has responsibility for national parks, and provincial, regional or local administrations have responsibility for the area outside the parks.

The long term success of protected areas must be seen in the light of the search for more sustainable patterns of development in general. Therefore, Management Plans should be integrated with or at least link to local development processes and the activities of other agencies and organisations working in the area. The aspirations and needs of the local communities around the protected area (as well as those living in it) must also be identified and addressed through the planning process and in the final plan.

Link to National Systems Plans, other planning and legislation

Management Plans should desirably be prepared within the context of a national systems plan for protected areas (see Davey, 1998). This will help ensure co-ordination with other national planning systems/agencies and with other protected areas. It will also provide strategic guidance for individual Management Plans. If no system plan has been developed, Management Plans should be linked to other relevant plans (e.g. local government plans, development plans) and legislation.

Protected area planning will often need to be consistent with parallel environmental protection policy, and policies related to heritage protection. Where significant new developments are planned or changes are proposed which may have broader wildlife or environmental impact, it may be necessary before implementation to meet the requirements of other legislation. Examples are the National Environmental Policy Act in the USA, the Environmental Protection and Biodiversity Conservation Act in Australia, and the European Birds and Habitats Directives.

A clear framework of approved policy

It is important that management planning be carried out within a framework of approved policies within the protected area agency. This framework should be sufficiently specific both to guide and set limits on different aspects of protected area management.

Without a clear policy framework to guide the development and implementation of Management Plans, managers for different protected areas may struggle to define their own policies for the same issues – not only duplicating effort, but perhaps also leading to potentially conflicting or inconsistent interpretations and directions.

Finally it should be said that planning is a lot like other "good" things: it's not worth much in the absence of sound governance and/or competent administration.

3.5 Resources, commitment and capacity

Identification of resources required

A clear process for integrating park planning with budgets and budgeting must be in place. Without this, the objectives for management cannot be reconciled with the 'costs' of achieving them. The plan then loses credibility as an effective instrument to guide the management of the protected area. Instead it becomes a 'wish list' of actions to be carried out if and when funds are available. If costs are ignored, the value of the planning effort and its results are diminished.

A detailed financial analysis of the impacts of the plan and of the resources required for its implementation should be prepared and included in an associated Business Plan. For government agencies, this would be prepared as a separate document. Recurring expenditure required to run the protected area should be linked to the annual budgeting process for the organisation, and additional capital required to carry out specific projects should be highlighted and sources of funding identified (for further advice on business planning for protected areas, see IUCN, 2000a).

Capacity for planning

The management planning process will run much more smoothly if an effort has been made to train and educate staff (especially protected area managers) on the planning process and to provide them with the skills required to participate in this task. Therefore building such capacity is a priority for management.

Management Plans can be prepared, either by using external consultants, or with internal expertise. There are some advantages to using external consultants to prepare plans (they can provide objectivity, professional expertise and a fresh insight, as well as a 'professionally presented' document). However, once the plan is prepared, the expertise and knowledge gained by the consultants leaves with them. Plans prepared in-house may take longer and look less 'polished', but the use of in-house staff can result in a greater sense of ownership as well as contributing to staff development.

Many larger organisations responsible for managing protected areas contain planning units or individual specialists to coordinate the planning process, and to provide support and training for staff involved in the process. Whether or not staff resources are dedicated primarily to planning, it is advisable that planning systems are designed and adopted by the managing organisation. These should identify exactly how plans will be prepared, monitored, implemented and amended, and who will be involved. An explicit budget commitment should be made for the preparation and implementation of plans

There is often a temptation to divert staff engaged in planning to more immediate tasks and high priority deadlines. To ensure that the planning output is timely and of high quality, planning staff should be quarantined from involvement in day-to-day management issues as far as possible. On the other hand they should be aware of such issues to ensure the plan is realistic and well focused.

Commitment and accountability

Commitment to implement the plan should be secured across the organisation. Staff responsible for the implementation of the plan must be identified, and activity monitored. The planning process is stronger, and staff more committed to it, when there is clear support from senior management. The planning effort will be undermined if planning is not seen as a corporate priority nor as a specific 'function' of the organisation. Resources and time will simply not be spent on it. Good planning processes and Management Plans are essential for agency and public accountability.

Interdisciplinary collaboration

There must be an effective partnership between all the staff concerned in management planning. It is especially important that contributors from the social and natural sciences work closely with each other and with the protected area managers themselves, both in preparing and implementing the plan. Failure to secure such co-operation will undermine planning and management.

3.6 Problems encountered in planning and implementation

The problems encountered in management planning tend to be of two kinds:

- those faced when preparing a Management Plan; and
- those faced in its implementation.

Problems mostly arise from a failure to address the issues outlined above. Some of the common difficulties faced and their causes are:

Problems at the planning stage

Difficulties include:

- lack of qualified park staff to carry out the planning process;
- a lack of funds and equipment;
- insufficient technical support and insularity of planners;
- negative perceptions of the protected area by local communities;
- external economic pressures, such as pressures to exploit the resources or features of the protected area; and
- poorly developed communications with the public and other stakeholders.

When such problems come to dominate debate, staff often lose the incentive, motivation or focus to become engaged in the planning process. Management planning may be side tracked and delays affect the production of the plan. This draws criticism from the public and further demotivates staff. When draft plans incorporate large amounts of superfluous explanatory material, they can become very large documents, tedious to read, and make consultation difficult with staff and especially the public. This detail may divert attention from key actions and priorities set out in the plan. There may also be confusion about the terms being used within the plan, and a real difficulty in defining a clear rationale within the document for the decisions made. All of this makes communication with staff and the public difficult.

Problems at the implementation stage

Problems encountered during the implementation of the plan may stem from weaknesses in the plan itself – in its content, style or remit, or by creating unreasonable expectations about what will be achieved – or they may be a function of the characteristics and culture of the organisation.

How the plan was prepared (who was involved, at what stage etc.) will often have an impact on whether the plan is later successfully implemented. Frequently encountered problems include:

- insufficient attention is given to budgetary questions (financial information is either not included, or bears very little relation to the funds likely to be available);
- unrealistic assumptions are made about the management capacity of the organisation;

■ poorly formulated objectives (these may be very generic, failing to bring out the particular features of the park – or they mix up ends and means);

■ vital details (such as the scope of the problems to be addressed) are deferred for further study although this may be difficult to avoid;

■ a failure to allocate responsibilities for implementing plans;

■ vague and unspecific commitments that do not provide a basis for on-the-ground action;

■ undue emphasis on certain aspects of management, such as tourism or recreation, which may divert resources away from other important aspects of the protected area;

■ financial, managerial or even political instability;

■ a failure to set out clear imperatives and priorities: many plans contain options or tentative 'recommendations' rather than firm decisions on what the organisation has decided to do, thus diminishing the authority of the plan; and

■ Management Plans that are impractical: they cannot be used as a basis for action.

Finally, if relevant managers have not been responsible for preparation of a Management Plan, or at least fully involved in its preparation, it is likely that they will feel very little 'ownership' for the final document and thus be less inclined towards implementing it. This will be especially true if there is a lack of accountability within the organisation and few internal systems in place for monitoring and reporting on work carried out.

3.7 Abbreviated forms of planning

In the event that time or resources do not allow a full Management Plan to be undertaken, it may nonetheless be possible to develop a shortened or abbreviated document. Guidance to assist in this process is provided in Chapter 7.

4. The management planning process

4.1 Overview of the process

Management planning is a continuous process – a 'circle' with three main elements:

1. Preparation of a Management Plan
2. Implementation of the plan
3. Monitoring and review of the plan.

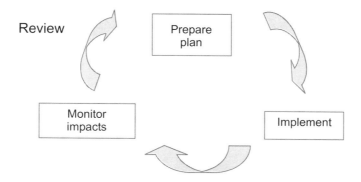

In this context, the actual process of planning can be broken down into 13 steps:

Fig. 2   Protected area management planning steps

1. Pre-planning – decision to prepare a Management Plan, appointment of planning team, scoping of the task, defining the process to be used

↓

2. Data gathering – issues identification, consultation

↓

3. Evaluation of data and resource information

↓

4. Identification of constraints, opportunities and threats

↓

5. Developing management vision and objectives

Fig. 2   Protected area management planning steps (cont.)

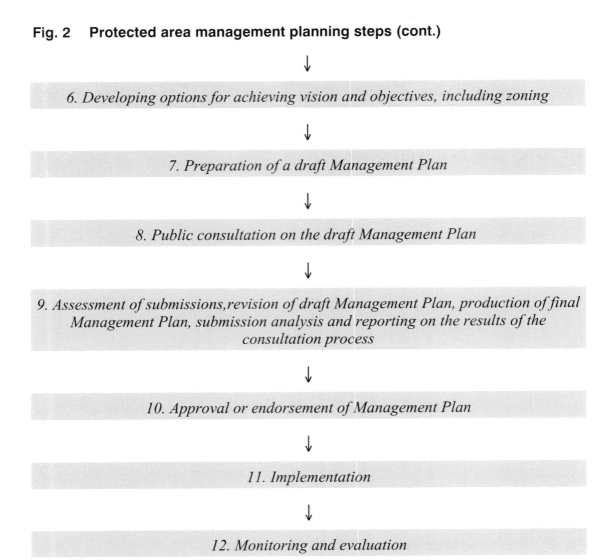

↓

6. Developing options for achieving vision and objectives, including zoning

↓

7. Preparation of a draft Management Plan

↓

8. Public consultation on the draft Management Plan

↓

9. Assessment of submissions, revision of draft Management Plan, production of final Management Plan, submission analysis and reporting on the results of the consultation process

↓

10. Approval or endorsement of Management Plan

↓

11. Implementation

↓

12. Monitoring and evaluation

↓

13. Decision to review and update Management Plan; accountability considerations

It is important that these steps are understood and carried out in a logical sequence. An orderly approach provides a more systematic and rational way of identifying and addressing all the factors involved. This is most important for complex cases. However, while a carefully phased sequence is desirable, experience suggests that a strictly sequential process may not always work best; this is particularly the case in the initial phases, when information gathering and evaluation are likely to take place almost simultaneously. Hence the work is likely to move forward opportunistically as delays are overcome and with several planning steps being worked on at once. Provided the overall framework is understood and complied with, this approach should not jeopardise the development of a good plan..

Fundamental to this process is 'feedback', which allows the planner to correct for future action in light of past experience. This feedback loop could also be thought of as a 'quality cycle', where the monitoring and review of the plan ensures that all parts are appropriate, realistic, efficient, economic and effective. It is the continuous nature of this process that ensures that the resulting management is flexible and can adapt to changing circumstances – and is thus of adequate quality.

4.2 Preparing a Management Plan

Step 1. Pre-planning phase

The pre-planning phase is one of the most important steps in the planning process. This stage defines what the process will achieve, how it will be carried out, timing considerations and who is to be involved. These decisions need to be made at the highest possible management level and are critical to starting the planning process on the right footing. This pre-planning phase generally includes the following steps:

1. *Clearly identify the purpose and management objectives of the protected area – and ensure that they are understood by all involved.* These broad objectives should have been set out in the legislation (or formal agreements designating the area), but it may be necessary to re-examine them and confirm their meaning, as they will set the direction of the plan from the start. The purposes should of course be reflected in the categorisation of the site within the IUCN protected area management categories system.

2. *Identify the steps to be followed in applying the planning process, their sequence and the methods to be used.* Many organisations have their own 'manual' or guidelines on the approach to be followed, which will have been designed to fulfil the needs and policies of the organisation. Otherwise, an approach should be designed which will best suit the protected area and its management context, but containing the basic stages of management planning (common to all planning processes).

   "With the many sound approaches to planning protected areas, it is not surprising that there are many 'right' answers. The best approach is the one most suited to the social and institutional environment of the country involved" (Child 1994).

3. *Determine who are the audiences for the plan.* Management Plans are prepared mainly for regular use by protected area managers, but they are not intended as detailed work programmes. Members of the public, the bureaucracy, commercial interests and neighbours are also important users. In some situations, traditional owners, local government and commercial operators can also be key users. The style of presentation adopted should reflect the most important user groups. In certain circumstances it may be necessary to produce the Management Plan in the official language(s) of the country and in local languages to meet local user requirements.

4. *Ensure that the protected area will be considered as a whole i.e. adopt a 'systems' approach'.* This recognises the importance of an analysis of separate issues, but stresses a **complete view** of all issues or 'systems' that are involved.

5. *Use an inter-disciplinary approach* – bringing experts and interested parties together to discuss the future management of the protected area.

   "In this approach, a problem is not disassembled (which is what happens in a multi-disciplinary approach). It is treated as a whole by repre-

sentation of different disciplines working the solution out together. This brings synthesis of knowledge in the sciences, technologies and humanities. Integration of disciplines yields broader synthesis of methods and knowledge and usually results in more complete and workable solutions" (Kelleher and Kenchington 1991).

6. *Identify a 'planning team'.* Management planning should be a 'team effort', but within this, one person should be given responsibility for production of the plan. This individual should be accountable to a clearly defined manager. If preparation is contracted out, decisions should be made as to how the contract will be managed to ensure that the plan delivers the requirements effectively. In such cases, it is essential to agree a 'brief' between the contractor and the organisation responsible for the management of the protected area before planning work commences. **NB: The Annex provides information on the skills required within a planning team.**

7. *Prepare and follow a well-laid out work schedule for the management planning process.* Project management techniques are often used to carry out this task. They help to organise and control the production of the Management Plan. The 'project' is defined as 'production of the plan' and a 'project manager' is identified to co-ordinate and oversee completion of the project.

8. *Identify a process for involving people (other than the planning team) in preparing the plan.* These will include other staff, experts, government officials, local communities and other affected parties. It should be clear to these and other interested parties when and how their participation will take place.

9. *Clarify and agree a procedure with senior management for the approval of the final Management Plan.* If the approval of external parties (e.g. funding bodies, advisory committees and government departments) is required, the procedures to be followed in achieving this should be identified and a timetable agreed to for the submission of a final version for approval.

Step 2. Data collection, background research and initial fieldwork

Planning and management should be informed by reliable data. There are two views about the relationship between data collection and setting management objectives:

1. That, through the collection and analysis of data, management objectives are refined and agreed upon after data is collected and analysed.

2. Management objectives are set for the area and these determine what data is collected.

In practice a protected area is established on the basis of an initial data set which is used to determine management objectives (e.g. protect rare habitat and species). Planning processes inevitably conclude more data are required before some management options can be evaluated and decided. In many cases there is a history of earlier planning or research efforts that help to identify the key topics where further data collection is required. Therefore data collection can almost always be informed to a considerable extent by the appropriate management objectives for the area. The stages involved are to:

i) gather available background information (historical data can be invaluable);

ii) carry out a field inventory to check the information (and to acquire additional data if required); and

iii) document it in the form of a description of the protected area (sometimes called a 'State of the Protected Area' report).

The information collected in this way should include both information about the area as it is, and about trends affecting it. The data should relate to both the physical aspects of the area, and to its social/cultural and economic significance (see **Guidelines** in Box 5).

Checking documentary information in the field is frequently not done because of the expense. It can be very useful, however, to confirm the accuracy of information; for historical sites, for example, it is an opportunity to examine the current physical state and to build up an understanding of how the site evolved and was used in the past. Moreover, evidence of meaningful data collection can help to build public confidence in the planning process.[1]

It may be necessary to define a long-term research programme for a site. This could apply to a range of factors where change over time is either evident or expected. The programme would form part of the Management Plan prescriptions.

It should not be expected that all the information collected for a protected area would necessarily be included in the Management Plan. A short summary should be included with the full text included as a companion document or, where this already exists, placed on the organisation's web site.

Step 2 is completed before moving through to the evaluation of this information, although in practice there is often some overlap, and iteration between these steps.

As always, time and resources will determine how much effort is put into this stage. However, the following **Guidelines** give advice on what data to collect:

Box 5. Guidelines on data collection

The following is a checklist of general types of information that may need to be collected:

- ecological resources and their condition
- cultural resources and their condition
- aesthetic aspect
- physical facilities (e.g. roads, buildings, easements, power and water supply)
- key features of the socio-economic environment[2]
- the capability of facilities in the protected area and its region to support existing and projected uses
- visitor characteristics and influence on the protected area
- predictions of the future condition of each of the above factors
- land uses and planning provisions of surrounding lands and any in-holdings or leases.

---

[1] Examples of how resource material is collected and presented can be found in the Management Plans for Norfolk Island National Park at www.ea.gov.au/parks/publications/norfolk-pom.html and for Booderee National Park at www.ea.gov.au/parks/publications/booderee-pom.html

[2] The need for socio-economic data will be greater in those IUCN protected area categories (e.g. V and VI) where there is a significant resident human population. Thus "in Category V protected areas, databases (are needed) on the state of the environment, the socio-economic conditions of local people and the nature and impact of any uses that affect these resources" (Phillips, 2002, p.107).

In its scope, the description should refer to the characteristics of the area itself, external factors which affect the area and factors which may become significant in the future. It should explain how things are changing, as well as their current impacts. It is important that the description identifies uses and activities both within and near the area that impair or adversely affect the protected area's values and resources, or visitor experiences, that the park was established to protect and provide.

In many cases it will be necessary for the planner to generate quantified information from surveys. This may include visitor numbers to the area, vehicle numbers, proportion of visitors travelling by bus, cars etc. The information may provide a base line or establish a trend. The gathering of this information requires a specialist approach, usually extended over 12 months or more: information gathering of this kind should take place well before the planning period. For the first Management Plan for an area, key management actions can be further data gathering, so that a future plan is better focused and targeted.

Guidelines on the information to include in the description are in Box 6. The type of information included will, of course, vary from protected area to protected area and depend on the characteristics of the area itself.

In addition to collecting site-related information, it is necessary to identify and understand the relevant government legislation affecting planning of the site. Applicable legislation may exist at all tiers of government; it should be closely considered to ensure compliance. As well as nature conservation laws, many others may affect the protected area, for example, legislation affecting water supply, cultural heritage, fishing, hunting, telecommunications, roads and electricity infrastructure.

Box 6.   Guidelines on the information to be included in the description

- Location (latitude and longitude)
- Area
- IUCN protected area management category
- Legal status, e.g. designation (both of the site and features within it) and relevant legislation
- Legal ownership, occupancy, access, tenure, access, other conditions and restrictions
- Addresses of the management agency and local management
- Organisational issues
- Current land use (including forestry, the extraction of other resources (eg gravel, sand, fish)
- Services in and to the area
- Main access routes
- Historical information (land use and landscape history, archaeology, buildings)
- Biological information (communities, flora and fauna)
- Physical information (climate, geology, geomorphology, hydrology, soil characteristics)
- Cultural and aesthetic information (landscape and landscape features, cultural associations)
- Socio-economic information (basic data and trends among local communities and their dependence on protected areas).

The planner should also be aware of the existence of any international obligations that affect the area concerned. These include sites which are already designated under international treaties like the World Heritage Convention and regional agreements (e.g. Natura 2000 in Europe) (see also Chapter 6). Planners should be aware that many sites not yet identified under international agreements have the potential to be so designated: the quality of the Management Plan may be a critical factor in deciding if they are eventually recognised in this way.

A particular challenge (and opportunity) arises in the case of protected areas that are on or near an international or provincial level boundary, adjoining another area that is – or might be – designated under separate legislation. IUCN strongly encourages transboundary co-operation in such circumstances (Sandwith *et al.*, 2001): it advises managers to "formulate joint or complementary Management Plans and facilitate joint management meetings on strategic transboundary elements of these plans" (ibid, p.28).

In a similar way, the planner needs to recognise that a range of other institutional factors may impact on the protected area and should be taken into account. This could include co-operation and agreements with local communities living in and near the protected area, natural resource management agencies, resource extraction corporations (mining, forestry etc.), and tourist organisations and businesses. The planner also needs to anticipate where potential issues may arise in future: for example to meet a particular revenue target or to achieve a specific wildlife protection outcome.

Guidelines on the preparation of a protected area description are set out in Box 7.

Box 7. *Guidelines* on preparing a protected area description

1. Identify gaps in information

For many protected areas, there may be little background information. Where this is the case, gaps in information should be highlighted within the description. Identification of gaps in knowledge is one of the main purposes of this stage of the process. Once highlighted, the need to obtain further information (or collate properly what already exists) may become an objective of the first plan for a protected area.

There may be times when a lack of information means that the site cannot be satisfactorily evaluated. If this is the case, it should be made clear. An interim Management Plan may be necessary while critical data are collected.

2. Do not postpone the planning process until all the information is available

The IUCN guidelines for the preparation of Management Plans for marine protected areas are adamant on this point: "it is nearly always a mistake to postpone a decision at one of the early decision-making stages until all the information needed for a later decision-making stage is obtained" (Kelleher 1999). There is a tendency for organisations to enter a 'decision-making paralysis' when faced with having to make decisions on tricky subjects without adequate information. Managers (and planners) rarely consider they have enough information and generally have to accept this situation: possible lack of information should not become an excuse for delaying the production of the plan:

"a competent plan can be developed from relatively simple descriptions of the physical, biological and socio-economic characteristics of an area. More sophisticated data add to the confidence of the manager or planner, but they rarely justify a

Cont.

Box 7. *Guidelines* **on preparing a protected area description (cont.)**

dramatic change of plan. The absence of site-specific information is not normally a good reason for postponing management in favour of more research" (Kelleher 1999).

3. Collate and include only RELEVANT information

Many Management Plans tend to become large, cumbersome documents – with the greatest weight in the descriptive section! The description should not be excessively detailed. The descriptive information in the plan should be **relevant** to the management of the protected area

4. Be objective – do not include 'value judgements'

The description should present factual information about the protected area, leaving value-laden statements to the 'evaluation' stage.

> *"As far as possible a site description should be neutral; value judgements should be avoided. However, there is no such thing as an entirely 'objective' description of a site. Some types of information, such as landscape assessment, are by their nature value based. They should still be done in a systematic way. Where subjective descriptions or judgements are included – you should say who made them"* (Clarke and Mount 1998).

5. Quantify and qualify the facts and identify the assumptions

When presenting facts, these should be quantified wherever possible, and the sources identified. However, rather than set down 'half facts' without qualification, include phrases such as 'to the best of our knowledge'.

> *"This is better than giving people with specialist knowledge sticks with which to beat the plan and, by implication but perhaps wrongly, criticise other parts"* (CCS 1989).

If there are inherent biases in information, these should be identified. Assumptions made should also be specified. Most descriptions will be based on some assumptions, especially where there are gaps in information, or where information is unobtainable, inconclusive, too expensive to collect or outside the scope of the plan. In such circumstances, assumptions should be clearly stated.

6. Keep it brief – use maps, references and appendices

Supporting information can be included in appendices, or simply referred to with references. Maps are another way of concisely presenting a lot of information. They can, for example, be used to illustrate/delineate geological formations, vegetation types, elevations, local climatic differences, location of major wildlife habitats, herd migration routes, recreation patterns, local settlement patterns, degrees of economic hardship and other factors relating to local communities and land uses.

7. Use local knowledge

When collecting information on the protected area and adjacent lands, local knowledge can be very valuable. Local people frequently know more than so-called experts. It should be possible to use, and even pay, local people to gather some data. This may be cost effective and may enhance their interest and involvement in the plan. The traditional knowledge of indigenous peoples regarding plants and animals and how they should be looked after should be drawn on where available.

Step 3. Evaluating the information

The purpose of this step is to identify and understand why the protected area is important. It helps to describe the 'values' associated with the protected area, explains why it was designated and identifies its benefits to society.

As more emphasis is placed on including local people and other 'stakeholders' in the planning process, it is important to have a mechanism through which the values they hold for the area can be identified and described.

Unless protected area values are understood, there is a risk that management actions, either deliberately or inadvertently, will affect not only the natural resources but also the social and economic situation, especially that of local people. Frequently the initial reasons for creating a protected area are subjective or poorly understood and badly communicated. Unless the Management Plan can document the inherent natural and cultural values, incompatible usage may continue, making it difficult to ensure its conservation into the future. Unless the preparation of Management Plans addresses the concerns of local people then their support will be impossible to secure.

The evaluation of values is a two-part process:

1. The identification of the **key features** or **exceptional values.** These are the features or values that must be protected and preserved to maintain the significance of the protected area. They may not be limited to those within the protected area boundary.

2. The development of a **succinct statement of significance** which explains the protected area's importance to society or particular interest groups. The statement of significance expands upon the identification of values by adding unique qualifiers and placing protected areas within their context at a regional, national and international level. Along with the protected area's broad purposes, this statement provides an important framework upon which the Management Plan should be based.

The significance of the protected area, including a view of its potential values, is basic to all the other assumptions about the site and decisions about the way it should be managed and used. Sometimes the founding legislation or legal agreement designating the protected area will mention its importance; more often, it will only be vaguely mentioned, if at all.

An essential part of carrying out an evaluation of any protected area is to define the criteria by which to identify and measure its natural, cultural and socio-economic values, now and in the future. However, many Management Plans fail properly to identify the existing and potential cultural, social and economic values of a protected area and tend to limit their analysis to the narrower aspects of ecological evaluation. It is unwise to overlook wider values, since this will affect the attitude of local peoples towards the protected area and can seriously undermine the planning process and the effectiveness of subsequent management.

The **Guidelines** in Box 8 list the factors to be considered when identifying the 'exceptional values' of a protected area.

Above all, the availability and evaluation of information about the protected area must be an open process and undertaken through wide consultation. However issues like the specific location of rare plants or animals should not be given too precisely.

31

> ### Box 8. **Guidelines** on criteria for exceptional value
>
> *In assessing the significance of a protected area, the planner should ask if the area contains:*
>
> - Outstanding examples of natural, scenic, geological, scientific, ecological, floral, faunal and recreational values (and if so, why)
> - Unique biological attributes, vegetation types and landforms (and if so, why)
> - Areas essential for protecting the ecological integrity of the protected area as a whole, (including areas critical for maintaining water flow and quality and the reasons why)
> - Areas and resources that are vital (economically, culturally or in other ways) to local communities
> - Areas and resources which provide essential services to people outside the park, especially where these have significant economic or political values
> - Rare and endemic plants and animals
> - Sensitive, threatened or endangered plants and animals and habitats
> - Resources which are unusually sensitive to human use
> - Outstanding examples of modified landscapes and evidence of sustainable use of natural resources
> - Major archaeological or historical sites
> - Major cultural sites
> - Features with world-wide recognition (e.g. as World Heritage).

Step 4. Identifying constraints, opportunities and threats

Before defining the specific management objectives for the protected area, the constraints on its management should be identified, as should any major threats to the area's values.

Some constraints are a function of the natural environment. Examples are the ecological processes which exist in the area, the presence of unique and vulnerable features, the relative rarity of the resource and any other aspects which may be identified.

Constraints may take other forms, such as:

- legal obligations;
- constraints of tenure;
- prior usage (for example an established fishery or mining operation);
- health and safety considerations;
- managerial constraints;
- priority activities and uses (which must be given precedence in the plan);
- obligations to neighbours, visitors etc.; and
- other policy considerations.

Threats to, or pressures on the protected area may be human-induced or natural, and may originate from within the protected area or from beyond its boundaries. Often they will manifest themselves in the form of social or economic demands upon the protected area.

Since planning is about the future, the factors which can affect the future of the protected area must be identified and evaluated. Whilst such prediction is at best uncertain, the identification of future trends in visitor use, economic and related pressures, and ecological change should be attempted. An understanding of the socio-economic environment is of particular importance. Predictions are not just about future threats – they may also help to identify opportunities for beneficial change, remediation or restoration (e.g. by reduction in pest numbers).

Once identified, the threats (and opportunities) should be clearly included in the Management Plan. Many practitioners include this information in the description, while others have a specific 'analysis' section of the plan for this purpose.

Several techniques are suggested for leading the planning team through the evaluation and identification of issues. For example, the TANAPA (Tanzania National Parks) management planning project prepared Management Plans for their national parks, using a 'Strategic Planning Process' (SPP). SPP uses interactive workshops to ensure the broadest level of involvement, input and support from a range of professionals and public. A 'nominal group process' was used to reach consensus in the identification and prioritisation of problems and issues, exceptional resource values and management objectives (Young, 1992).

Step 5. Developing management vision and objectives

A long-term vision
The management planning process should develop and articulate an ideal condition, state or appearance for the future of the protected area. In some plans, this future is defined within goals or aims for the protected area; in others, within 'long-term objectives'. In some more recent plans, it has taken the form of a 'vision statement'.

Vision statements describe the desired or envisaged result of the policies for the conservation of the protected area. Without this 'vision', a plan may have little coherent direction. Its purpose is to provide a focus or direction for management objectives. Importantly a vision statement should be aspirational.

Whatever the form of wording of the vision for the protected area, it should:

■ describe the kind of protected area that the plan is seeking to achieve in the long term. This will help people to understand what it is hoped the area will be like in the future, the reasons for this, and the action needed to achieve the vision;

■ be a long-term statement which is unlikely to change significantly over time. It should therefore provide continuity in the process of managing the park in a sustainable way; and

■ include environmental, recreational, cultural and social and economic aspects of the protected area.

Definition and role of 'objectives'
Objectives follow from the management vision. They are more specific statements of intentions, setting out the conditions that management aims to achieve. They are thus statements of 'outcomes' rather than how to achieve them.

To the extent possible, these objectives should be listed in priority order to guide subsequent decisions. Objectives can be contentious, creating difficulties within the agency charged with the management of the protected area, the community or the users.

While each group, for example, may agree with the long-term vision, it is frequently the case that objectives and the means of achieving them will be perceived differently, along with the order of priorities. As an example, user groups may agree that protection of a site in a natural condition is a valid vision, provided the area still remains available for recreational use. Others may wish to exclude the more excessive forms of recreational use, such as off-track 4wd excursions, claiming this damages the natural qualities of the area and its ambience. There is therefore a need to reconcile the different objectives through appropriate planning responses.

In developing initial management objectives, a three-stage approach can be used:

- design overall management objectives;
- develop issue-specific management responses; and
- prepare initial management options.

Describing and prioritising management objectives may be an important part of the planning and consultation processes. Within Management Plans, objectives tend either to relate to 'key features' of the protected area (defining how these will be conserved), or to important areas of management activity. Typically objectives would be formulated to cover the following:

- habitat and species management;
- research, survey and monitoring;
- infrastructure including communications;
- visitor use and facilities;
- education and training;
- social and cultural features;
- income generation;
- protected area services; and
- administration.

The management objectives for the appropriate IUCN Protected Area Management Category (see Section 2.1 and IUCN, 1994) should be taken into account in formulating specific management objectives and their priority order.

Characteristics of 'good' (well-written/designed) objectives

Well-stated objectives are critical in determining whether a Management Plan is effective. If they are poorly formulated and expressed, or provide only vague guidance for

---

Box 9. Guidelines for writing objectives

Management Plan objectives should be:

- Precise/specific
- Achievable and realistic
- Time-related
- Measurable
- Reflect park purpose, significance and exceptional values
- Spell out the ends desired, but not the means to those ends
- Adequately address the issues
- Accompanied by a rationale
- Written in priority order.

---

managers, the plan will lose credibility and the resulting management may fail to deliver the desired vision for the protected area or meet the expectation of stakeholders.

Guidelines for expressing objectives are summarised in Box 9, and developed further below.

■ **Precise/specific**

Effective management is not only about achieving objectives in general, but also about achieving each objective individually. Without precise and measurable objectives, it is difficult to determine just what is to be done or how to do it.

A typical weakness of some Management Plans is to be too "aspirational" in their objectives. While aspiration is important it is best captured in the vision statement. Management objectives should be written so they are difficult to misinterpret.

■ **Achievable and realistic**

It must be possible to achieve the management objectives for the protected area recognising the constraints faced by managers. For this reason, the aspirations expressed in the vision will need to be translated into more practical terms and address the prevailing practical realities. Once more: "no wish lists".

■ **Time-related**

To the extent possible, objectives should be time-related. While this is more realistically achieved with a planning horizon of 5–10 years, the principle still applies to plans with longer timescales. Managers' accountability to stakeholders should be measured by the timeliness of the actions undertaken to implement the plan.

■ **Measurable**

Managers must be able to tell whether management activities are achieving the desired results as this is an important measure of success. It will only be possible to identify this if objectives are quantified, or referred to as an outcome that can in some way be measured. Management objectives must be written with this in mind.

This is not easy and often there is not enough knowledge of the ecological features, for example, to do this. However first steps towards a measurable approach are fundamental and can be used to identify research and information requirements.

An approach which has been used for many designated nature conservation sites in the UK is called 'common standards monitoring' (CSM). CSM has been developed to help standardise monitoring of important sites:

"In this approach, only the features for which the site was designated are monitored. These are then classified as being either in favourable con- dition or as being in unfavourable condition. In this way it is possible to categorise any feature as either meeting its conservation objective (favourable condition) or not (unfavourable condition)" (Alexander and Rowell 1999).

This approach may work well for those things that can be easily quantified, but does not adapt easily to more intangible notions, such as natural beauty or visitor experience. In such cases, public attitude surveys based on direct and indirect indicators may be used. For example a survey of visitors will indicate their underlying satisfaction with the management of a protected area and can be used as an indicator of success. By seeking a response to questions such as "would they visit the park again?" or "what feature of the park did the visitor like best?" a profile of the important but intangible values of the park can be obtained, the outcomes assessed, and these used to guide future planning.

■ **Reflect park purpose, significance and exceptional values**

The objectives should not restate the purposes of the protected area but set out important aspects that will accomplish this purpose.

■ **Spell out the ends desired, but not the means to those ends**

This is a common fault, probably because identifying a desired 'end' is more difficult than stating how it will be achieved. Objectives should not describe the programmes, actions and support facilities needed to achieve these desired conditions, which are tasks that should be addressed later in the process. For example if an objective is to protect a critical habitat, it should refer to the threats that **need** to be addressed (fire, pests) but not **how** these will be addressed.

■ **Adequately address the issues**

Objectives need to respond to the issues that have been identified in previous steps of the planning process. All key issues should be addressed in at least one objective: however, the objectives do not need to address each issue separately. There are likely to be some management objectives that do not correspond specifically to an issue but nonetheless describe a condition desired in the park.

■ **Accompanied by a rationale**

During the decision-making process, and in the body of the draft and final plans, the reasoning behind the choice of objectives should be explained. This will help communicate the significance of the Management Plan and its objectives.

■ **Written in priority order**

Objectives should be presented in priority order to ensure there is a clear understanding about the most important aspects to be included and accomplished through the Management Plan.

Limits of acceptable change and thresholds of potential concern

Increasingly, in an effort to try to include more specificity and targets within objectives, 'limits of acceptable change' (LACs) are being developed for key features of a protected area (and for their attributes). The original use of the LAC approach was in determining recreational carrying capacity of wilderness areas, but the benefits of this approach are now recognised in the wider planning process.

LACs are designed to identify the point at which changes in the resource brought about by another management objective have exceeded levels that can be tolerated. A LAC contains 'standards' that express **minimally acceptable conditions** (but not desired conditions or unacceptable conditions). The implication is that conditions can be allowed to deteriorate until this minimally acceptable condition is in danger of being reached. At this point, management should intervene to prevent further deterioration.

Obviously monitoring is needed to measure the condition and trigger intervention if limits are exceeded, or in danger of being breached.

LACs can help add specificity to objectives by:

■ prescribing quantifiable limits for selected ecological parameters as an alternative to a condition of, for example, 'naturalness' (which is open to interpretation); and

■ providing a basis for measuring some aspects of management success and staff capability.

LACs are only useful when there is conflict between two or more objectives, **and** where compromise is possible. That is why it works well in many recreational carrying capacity situations. For example, Objective 1 may be to allow access to a trail; Objective 2 may be to provide opportunities for quiet recreation. A threshold number of people on the trail has been identified as the maximum possible before quiet recreation becomes compromised (the LAC). In the case of this trail, the managers decide that Objective 2 should take precedence. If in achieving Objective 1, so many people come on to the trail that standards defining 'quiet recreation' are exceeded, Objective 2 is clearly being compromised. Since Objective 2 takes precedence, action should be taken to restrict access to the trail.

Guidelines on the use of LACs (outside a wilderness situation) are set out in Box 10. However planners should develop a full understanding of the LAC approach and its relevance to their management needs before embarking on what can be a complex process. It is not always an easy or appropriate technique to apply. It certainly will not work for issues where the desirable or acceptable future conditions are hard to determine and may change over time.

Box 10. Guidelines: Applications of LAC beyond wilderness recreation

It may be possible to apply LACs in conditions where:

1. Goals are in conflict;

2. A hierarchy of goals exists, so that one or more goals can be said to constrain the other goals; or

3. It is possible to develop measurable standards.

LAC is of little value if:

1. There is no conflict between goals. In this case, managers should strive for desired conditions rather than acceptable conditions;

2. Managers are unwilling to compromise one of the goals (where this happens, it is better to strive for the desired conditions of the 'uncompromisable' goal); or

3. Both goals are considered equally important.

Source: Cole and Stankey (1997).

South Africa National Parks has developed a similar method for determining when management intervention is required in a certain situation. This system is based on **"Thresholds for Potential Concern"** or TPCs and was first used to guide the management of the riverine systems within Kruger National Park. The TPC system has been extended to cover all terrestrial ecological features within the park and TPCs form an important part of the existing Kruger Management Plan (SANP 1997).

TPCs define the 'desired state' of a feature by identifying an upper and lower level along a continuum of change. They are designed to act as 'amber lights' – so that when a threshold is reached, or when modelling predicts it will be reached, managers are prompted to carry out an assessment of the causes and extent of change. This assessment is then used to decide whether action is needed to correct the change, or whether the TPC needs to be re-calibrated. Re-calibration builds in an opportunity for managers and scientists to use new knowledge about a system or ecological feature so as to change the TPC if it has been set at an inappropriate level.

Both LACs and TPCs should be set out in an operational plan (work plan, action plan or implementation plan) that outlines the necessary management actions, the timetable for them and the responsibility for action. Financial information illustrating the costs of implementing the work plan may also be attached.

Step 6. Identifying and evaluating options including zoning

With management objectives in place, the next step is to work out how the objectives will be achieved. As there are often several ways in which this can be done, the range of options for management actions should be identified, and the appropriate ones chosen. Management zones can be used to meet multiple management objectives.

Guidelines for identifying and evaluating options are set out in Box 11.

Box 11. **Guidelines** for identifying and evaluating management options

First:

Ask these questions:

- In what different ways might the objectives be achieved?
- What possible options exist?
- What combination of options fit together to form coherent plans?

In answering such questions, the planner should:

- repeatedly refer back to, and check options against objectives, to ensure that any option does contribute to achieving what was originally intended; and look forward and work out the interaction of options – and the design and management implications of possible solutions;
- be aware of constraints and evaluate each option to see if it is realistic (inspiration, intuition, lateral thinking and originality have a special place here); and
- develop options to the stage where they have spatial expression and the management implications of each are clear (although it is wasteful to develop each option to detailed design).

Then:

Ask these questions:

- Which options represent the best value for money?
- What is the 'best' set of options?
- Which options meet pre-agreed criteria?

In answering such questions, the planner may wish to consider:

- which alternative meets the objective best;
- whether the alternative will work;
- whether each scheme is financially feasible;
- how acceptable the options are to politicians and the wider public; and
- who wins and who loses– that is which groups of society will benefit from the scheme and which will suffer disadvantages.

From the process set out in Box 11, it should be possible to identify the precise actions that will be required to fulfil each management objective, in the most appropriate way.

Zoning – and its benefits

Management Plans for protected areas may identify different 'management zones' – that is geographical areas within which similar management emphases are applied and similar levels of use permitted and different uses segregated. Zoning is a widely used and long established method of organising resource information, and guiding management tasks, in a structured way.

"Zoning defines what can and cannot occur in different areas of the park in terms of natural resources management; cultural resources management; human use and benefit; visitor use and experience; access; facilities and park development; maintenance and operations. Through management zoning the limits of acceptable use and development in the park are established" (Young and Young 1993).

Zones identify **where** various strategies for management and use will best accomplish management objectives to achieve the desired future of the protected area. Within each zone, the management prescriptions should be reasonably uniform but may differ in type or intensity from those in the other zones in order to accommodate multiple objectives.

Typically zoning will be used to:

■ provide protection for critical or representative habitats, ecosystems and ecological processes;

■ separate conflicting human activities;

■ protect the natural and/or cultural qualities while allowing a spectrum of reasonable human uses; and

■ enable damaged areas to be set aside to recover or be restored.

Zoning may also be invoked on a temporal basis where an area is managed according to the time of day, days of the week or months of the year, to allow for cultural events, acknowledge seasonal changes or by reference to some other trigger or causal event (e.g. breeding seasons).

By providing control over areas designed to meet different conservation and use objectives, zoning is a widely used and useful tool but zonation of a protected area is not always required. Zoning should simplify not complicate management.

Types of management zones in IUCN Protected Area Categories I–IV

Many different kinds and names of management zone are used in protected area planning. However, it is possible to identify several common types of zone used in the more strictly protected categories of protected area (I-IV):

■ **Special and/or unique values zone**

This zone should contain outstanding, special or unique values – e.g. historic sites; important natural areas such as wetlands, salt marshes, estuaries or key marine areas such as spawning aggregations, which should be given priority for protection. Those parts of protected areas that are inhabited by indigenous peoples, or which are important as anthropological or unique cultural niches, should also be protected by zoning that recognises these special values and limits or excludes unwanted visitation.

■ **Primitive/wilderness zone**

In this zone, roads and infrastructure development should be excluded, and manipulative management techniques normally prohibited. Natural processes dominate. Under normal circumstances, trails and perhaps a few, basic camping sites would be permitted – but their nature, number and extent should be strictly controlled. Sometimes these areas are called "core zones", since they are likely to have the best preserved natural values.

■ **Limited development zone**

Limited development would be permitted in this zone, but must not be detrimental to the special or unique values of the park. An important purpose of this zone is to cater for certain types of recreational use, thereby relieving pressures on primitive or wilderness areas. In all cases the development should have minimal impact and serve only the immediate users of the designated area.

■ **Intensive development/services zone**[3]

In many more strictly protected areas, this zone would be inappropriate. Its purpose is to accommodate major roads, hotels, accommodation and service facilities. The goal should be to avoid creating zones of this kind in or near areas containing special or unique values or that exemplify an ecosystem type etc. In many protected areas, the current trend is to move more intensive development to areas outside the boundary altogether. While this may increase servicing costs in the protected area, experience has found that it:

■ frees management time and resources;

■ is usually less detrimental to the protected area's natural values; and

■ avoids the creation and siting of secondary service industries or activities within the protected area.

Arguments in favour of allowing more intensive development within protected areas can also be well founded, particularly where the protected areas are large. These include:

■ having stronger control over the design, use and siting of the facilities, and their impacts;

■ allowing visitors to maximise their time in the protected area;

■ enabling a better spread of visitor and recreational uses; and

■ benefits from increased user and visitor fees.

■ **Zoning for traditional and indigenous users**

Many protected areas provide zones for use by indigenous and traditional users. Many other protected areas around the globe, including Kakadu National Park and the Great Barrier Reef Marine Park, make provision within zones allocated for this purpose. Where appropriate, limited development may occur to provide basic amenities for the traditional users.

---

[3] For more detail, see Chapters 5 and 7 of Eagles *et al.* (2002).

Types of management zones in IUCN Protected Area Categories V and VI

Within protected landscapes and multiple use areas it is more likely that zoning will need to be employed to accommodate the varying economic, cultural and resource uses that occur. Zoning in Category V areas will normally be achieved using land use plans reflecting geographically based policies for different parts of the landscape or seascape. Thus one part of area may be designated for economic activities and others conserved to protect natural values. A critical factor in the success of zoning plans is to ensure that adequate public consultation has been undertaken in their development and the outcomes are accepted by affected parties. Processes for considering applications for development and the regulatory arrangements that apply need to be taken into account in defining zones, and what is and is not permitted in them.[4]

Zoning is a fundamental planning tool for multiple use Category VI protected areas. Zoning sets the boundaries for activities permitted within the protected area and as such determines the different patterns of usage. The zones and the policies which apply should be described in full detail in the Management Plan. In large multiple use protected areas, such as the Great Barrier Reef Marine Park, this part of the Management Plan is of critical importance as it reflects the activities that can be undertaken, eg commercial fishing, tourism and related activities and research.

Subzones

Unique situations, if not accommodated in another way, may require special attention by the use of subzones or modifiers. e.g. 'Time-and-Place' zoning. This may include vehicle and boating access, visitation times and seasonal considerations.

Identifying zones and preparing a zoning plan

There is no set formula for identifying management zones. The planner and the planning team should start with the relevant management objectives. Then criteria for zoning designations should be agreed, based on the objectives for the area and within the scope of the options developed. The zones are identified using the best information available and the professional judgement of the interdisciplinary planning team.

Factors to take into account may include:

- protection of exceptional resource values;
- constraints imposed by the landscape and other ecological determinants e.g. slope, soil type and hydrology, landscape values;
- provision of a diverse range of appropriate visitor use experiences;
- elimination or minimisation of uses and activities that either damage park resources or create an undue burden on park management;
- the capability of the protected area to support different types of desired uses and development;
- the results of public participation or consultation – prior to the preparation of the plan;
- government policy and decisions regarding land use; and
- established uses by local people and communities.

---

[4] For a fuller description, see Phillips (2002).

Computer generated spatial representations can frequently be performed where appropriate resource information is available (and occurs at the right scale). Different overlays of information can be integrated to assist the planner in arriving at the optimum balance between conservation and use, thus meeting the objectives established for the area.

Care should be taken not to create too complex a pattern of zoning. The adoption of multiple zones with only slight differences between them can be confusing to the public and management alike. The aim should be to use the minimum number of zones needed to achieve the management objectives. Where zoning is used, zones should be able to be easily identified by visitors and to enable them to know what zone they are in and therefore what constraints apply. This is particularly important for zoning in open waters of marine reserves.

Step 7. Integration into a draft plan

The integration of all of the above planning elements into a single document will result in a draft Management Plan.

There are many possible ways to present a Management Plan, and many variations in content, sequence and level of detail can be found. The form of the plan will be a function of the budget, the management philosophy, the remit of the management agency and the aims of the Management Plan. But while there is thus no standard format for a Management Plan and no 'right' or 'wrong' approach, the content and structure of a plan should always reflect the needs of the site, the purposes and requirements of its managers and the availability of resources.

For a major national park, it would be expected that the plan would be a larger more complex document than that for smaller or less significant protected areas where it will often be appropriate to produce a simpler document. It may be difficult to decide how much information should be provided. Again, with a large national park, this can be extensive and may form a large part of the plan, though current practice is usually to publish this material as an Annex, or separate document, keeping the plan itself focussed on matters concerning the management and use of the area. Topics of only limited relevance should receive only brief discussion – always place the emphasis on the significant issues that have a bearing on the management objectives and achieving results.

Basic elements of a Management Plan

Even though there is no such thing as a standard format for a Management Plan, plans tend to contain certain standard elements. These are outlined below in Box 12. The guidance assumes that the plan's content will reflect the thought processes used during its preparation. Planning should be a logical process and – when prepared in this way – most plans will flow sensibly from beginning to end. They start with an introduction to the protected area and a discussion of its importance and the factors affecting it, take the reader through the formulation of a 'vision' for its future management and end with prescriptions about how this vision will be achieved, and how managers and others will assess the effectiveness of the plan towards the end of its life.

Box 12. *Guidelines* on the content of Management Plans

The elements **most commonly found** in Management Plans are outlined below. These are not necessarily 'chapter headings' within a plan, although they may be. They may occur as headings in the plan, be 'lumped together' or be split into smaller sections, depending on the complexities and characteristics of the area, the planning process used and the needs of the manager. Some of these elements may be absent, or additional ones added. They closely mirror the steps in the process used.

Executive summary
This summarises essential issues within the plan and relevant decisions. This is important as many of the final decision-makers will not have time to read and digest supporting detail.

Introduction
This states the purpose and scope of the plan, and provides an explanation of the purpose for which the protected area was established (including any legislative basis) and the authority for plan development. It *may* also contain some basic summary information about the protected area, such as its location, size, primary resources and values.

Description of the protected area
This summarises relevant descriptive information about the protected area. It normally includes a summary account of the resources (features) of the area (natural, cultural, historical and socio-economic), how it is used, and its legal and management framework. It can be equally important to state what the plan does not cover.

Evaluation of the protected area
This identifies why the protected area is important, and explains the values associated with it. It frequently takes the form of a 'Statement of Significance' or Key Features of the area.

Analysis of issues and problems
This section contains an analysis of the constraints and opportunities affecting the area and a statement of the principal threats to its conservation, management and maintenance. Also any impacts (internal or external) on the important features of the area should be stated, along with any other management considerations.

Vision and objectives
This contains a broad, long-term vision for the protected area, which may take the form of goals, and a 'vision statement'. Any guiding policies for management can be included here. A set of objectives is provided. These are specific statements outlining what is to be achieved by management in the timeframe of the plan. A rationale for the objectives is often included and provides valuable justification of the decisions made during the planning process. Limits of Acceptable Change (LACs) may be provided for objectives.

Cont.

Box 12. *Guidelines* on the content of Management Plans (cont.)

Zoning plan	If different management zones are required, a zoning plan can be prepared to illustrate the boundaries, classification and management and other activities allowed or prohibited for each zone. Sub-objectives for each zone can also be provided. The zoning scheme can be included in the Management Plan, or presented separately. In many cases, the zoning plan will be prepared to inform the Management Plan; or it may already exist. Its findings are then summarised within the Management Plan. Specific constraints and conditions applying in each zone must be clearly described.
Management actions (prescriptions)	This contains the specific actions to be carried out in order to achieve the objectives. It commonly includes: ■ list of management actions/activities required (often called prescriptions); ■ schedule or work plan identifying when each action will be carried out and by whom (this may be a separate document); ■ priority activities identified; and ■ staff and finances required to carry them out (costings). If this section of the plan is to be very detailed, it can further break prescriptions down into 'projects', each of which is a detailed action. An explanation as to how these should be carried out can also be given. More commonly, the information in this section may not be detailed, but will be supplemented by separate annual operational or work plans, which will contain detailed costings and instructions.
Monitoring and review	This section outlines how implementation of the plan will be monitored, and when and how a review of the plan will be carried out. It will include the indicators against which the performance of the protected area will be measured.

Variations

It is not unusual to find a Management Plan that closely resembles the headings above – with the plan mirroring the steps in the planning process. However, many planners find it more effective, especially for complex and multi-purpose sites, to adopt headings that relate more closely to the broad **purposes** of the area (and/or its managing organisation). This is especially the case for the part of the plan that deals with policies, objectives, zones and management actions. In such cases, the plan may set out a set of management programmes dealing with:

■ Management to conserve biodiversity;
■ Management of the physical environment;
■ Management of biological components;
■ Community conservation programmes;

- Visitor facilities and protected area development;
- Protected area administration;
- Research and information; and
- Evaluation and review.

Such a structure aids communication and focuses the reader on how specific functions (for example, the conservation or public access purposes of a national park) will be achieved.

Such an approach is taken in Mexico, where the contents and format of Management Plans are decreed by legislation. In this case, there are seven set 'management programmes' covering:

(i)   conservation;

(ii)   sustainable social development;

(iii)   scientific research and environmental monitoring;

(iv)   legal framework;

(v)   administration;

(vi)   direction and coordination; and

(vii) operations.

Each management programme contains objectives, problems and strategies, actions and activities to be developed, and details of infrastructure, equipment and human resources required.

Management Plans for the national parks in England and Wales are also written to this sort of format, where the main chapter headings echo the broad purposes of the parks, see Box 13.

Box 13. Contents of a National Park Plan (England and Wales)

1. Introduction
2. Vision for the park
3. Conservation
    a. Natural environment
    b. Conservation of cultural heritage
4. Promoting understanding and enjoyment
    a. Recreation management
    b. Promoting understanding
5. Economic and social well-being of local communities
6. Development planning and development control
7. Park-related themes/policies for particular geographical areas
8. Implementation: applying policies in specific areas of the park: management, administration and resources
9. Monitoring and review

Source: Countryside Commission (1997).

In Tanzania, too, protected area 'plans of action' are presented under headings which relate broadly to the purposes of the protected area – see Box 14.

Box 14.   Contents of a [general] Management Plan – Tanzania

1.   Statement of park significance and purpose

2.   Analysis of issues and problems

3.   Description of exceptional resources and values

4.   List of management objectives describing the desired future of the park

5.   Plan of action that includes: zoning scheme with specific actions and determinations of limits of acceptable use and development for each zone; interrelated actions for:

- Resource protection and management
- Visitor use and development
- Land protection and boundary changes
- Cooperation with associated local and district interests
- Visitor experience, use and interpretation
- Accessibility for disabled visitors
- Park operations and environmental assessment of the plan
- Listing of plan implementation priority and funding packages

Source: Young and Young (1993).

A slightly different approach, used by the National Trust for Scotland and the Countryside Council for Wales (CCW), is to provide a management programme for each **key feature** of the area (see Alexander 1996). Such a key feature could be a habitat (e.g. woodland), a particular species, or archaeological sites or buildings. For each of these (or groups of them with similar characteristics and management needs) a management rationale, objectives and prescriptions are provided. CCW also identifies 'attributes' for each key feature and uses these to set limits of acceptable change. Thus in this type of Management Plan, the key features on the site dictate the headings.

Each of these variations in format has been developed and designed to meet the needs of the particular management organisation – and particularly to provide a document which most **clearly communicates** the management intent to all involved. Such variations in format are evidence that planners often seek one that suits their needs. Once developed, however, it is common for organisations to adopt their own 'standardised approach' as this can be stored as a template on computer disc and then used as a 'checklist' for all plans. A standard format can also help staff to become familiar with a plan and find information quickly and easily. It also helps achieve consistency across an agency, and assist in agency-wide reporting

Whatever design is chosen, it is advisable to be pragmatic rather than aiming for 'perfection'. Sophistication and detail can gradually be added to a plan through update and revision at a later stage. Some further **Guidelines** on the form of Management Plans are at Box 15.

Box 15. *Guidelines* on good practice in writing the Management Plan

- ■ Use a simple clear style with user friendly language
- ■ Place the protected area in its regional, national and international context
- ■ Identify and focus on the significant values and issues
- ■ Identify the criteria adopted in establishing the vision, management objectives, issues, options and zoning to ensure there is full understanding among the public and staff
- ■ Identify the criteria by which the performance of management under the plan will be assessed
- ■ Fully acknowledge public suggestions and consultation

Internal agency review

As the draft plan takes shape, it is useful to circulate the text internally within the management agency for comment. This provides the opportunity for staff with an interest in the management prescriptions to comment before any public consultation. It also helps pick up drafting inconsistencies, and may generate suggestions for improvements in presentation and content.

Step 8. Public consultation, including public exhibition of the draft plan

The opportunity for the general public and stakeholders to review the draft Management Plan and provide comment is a vital step in the management planning process. Chapter 5 further addresses this issue.

How public comment is sought will vary from agency to agency, and country to country. Each situation is different. However there will generally be two scenarios:

- ■ where the process for public consultation is predetermined; and
- ■ where the agency is free to determine its own course of action.

Where a formal consultation process is laid down, the agency must of course follow this. This would usually involve placing public notices to inform interested parties that the draft plan is available for viewing and where a copy can be obtained. The notice will also provide the deadline by which comments should be received and include advice as to where they should be sent. A contact person and phone number will generally also be provided.

The above is however only a minimum requirement. It will normally need to be accompanied by public meetings, media interviews, displays in public places and posting on the Internet. It is important for the public and stakeholders to have the opportunity to understand what is being proposed and to provide meaningful comment. Verbal comments should be noted and where possible attributed to the speaker. Comments in writing should also be invited as part of the process. The effort made to communicate with interested parties should recognise the likely level of interest in the plan.

The question of whether charges should be levied for making draft plans should be decided in accordance with an agency's policy. However the public are more likely to respond where the draft can be provided to them free of charge and this is recommended in order to achieve the best possible response rate.

Where the public consultation process is not laid down, the agency or management authority may decide its own course of action. While the above is considered the minimum requirement to be met, other steps might include:

- facilitating meetings of special interest groups to resolve conflicting requirements;
- facilitating direct consultations between planners and individuals/organisations;
- referring public submissions to external advisory groups e.g. consultative committees comprising community leaders/representatives for advice;
- formally involving independent statutory advisory committees in assessing plans and public submissions; and
- accepting input through political processes, particularly over more difficult issues.

The length of time required to ensure public comment varies. Three months would generally be a minimum requirement but should be extended if required to meet the needs of the public to have their say. Realistically six months may be the minimum required where a large protected area is involved or the issues are complex. Frequently additional time is requested by community groups and non-government organisations to review the draft and to provide comment. It becomes a matter of judgment then for the management agency to decide on the benefits of receiving late comment as against the need to move the plan to the next phase. The key point is that the Management Plan should be fully debated while in draft form, so that the final document adequately reflects the values and issues generated through the participation programme and establishes a sense of ownership. To achieve this a flexible approach needs to be taken on the time given to this step.

Box 16. *Guidelines* for consultation on the draft Management Plan

It is essential that the consultation processes create confidence among all stakeholders. This requires that the agency:

- identify all the stakeholders;
- approach all of them on the basis of equality and transparency;
- produce materials that are informative, clear and user-friendly;
- use a variety of culturally appropriate means to seek views ;
- emphasise the *draft* nature of proposals;
- be ready to revisit any proposal;
- keep a complete and documented record of all comments, and log all contacts;
- ensure that all requests for meetings, materials etc. are responded to promptly;
- make sure that every view has been considered, whether it is adopted or not;
- allow time so that people do not feel rushed by the process, but not so much that they lose interest;
- engage in further consultation if changes in the plan are envisaged that will affect other stakeholders than those seeking these changes;
- feedback the results of consultation to all who commented; and
- above all treat the stakeholders as essential partners in the conservation of the protected areas, not as obstacles.

Source: Adapted from Phillips (2002).

Box 16 suggests **Guidelines** on how this process of consultation should be conducted: it is adopted from guidance about Category V protected areas but the advice is relevant to other categories of protected areas.

Step 9. Revision of draft and production of final plan

This step in the process involves revision of the draft, taking into account the comments received from stakeholders and the public. Good practice requires that all written comments received, and those noted at public meetings etc., should be recorded and considered. Even if not incorporated into the final version, it would be appropriate for the planning team to summarise each comment received and include these as an annex to the published Management Plan, or to make it a separate document.

The planning team will be required to exercise judgment of the highest order in considering which comments to accept. Comments from user groups and stakeholders will tend to focus on single issues rather than the plan as a whole. The views of a particular group, however strongly advocated, should not be allowed to put at risk other elements of the plan.

It may be helpful to prepare a report on consultations to accompany the final plan. This report will detail how the comments received have been taken into account and indicate why some comments have not been used. It will help the public and stakeholders to understand the final version of the plan and appreciate how the management actions included in it have been arrived at.

The final published version of the Management Plan may take many forms. Usually it will be printed in hard bound copy and should be made available as a public document in saleable form. The print run will of course be determined by the size of the audience. Often it helps to produce a summary leaflet version for wider distribution, perhaps free of charge. The plan might also be posted on the agency's web site and made available for downloading. It may be useful to produce loose leaf versions of the Management Plan for agency staff, thereby providing them with ready access to frequently used sections.

Step 10. Approval of plan

This is a procedural step involving submission of the final plan for approval by the competent authority. Procedures will vary from country to country, but in most cases there will be a formal process of adoption or approval to give authority to the plan, often laid down in legislation and clearly documented.

For example in Australia, federal national parks Management Plans are required to be submitted to the Minister for Environment and Heritage for approval. The plan is also tabled in both houses of Parliament for a statutory period of 15 sitting days during which time Members may raise objections, or seek clarification in relation to the document.

Step 11. Implementation of the Management Plan

The Management Plan sets out actions to be implemented. These should be realistic and necessary for the management of the protected area. They should not be wish lists or include items which do not relate to the management objectives. This process gives clear legal authority to the Plan and provides a strong foundation for compliance and enforcement actions.

Two approaches are in general use: either

- the plans do not include detailed resource and financial information for each year; or

- the plans include information of this kind.

The reasons for adopting the first approach are complexity and scope of the tasks, and that it is difficult to forecast costs accurately more than a year or two in advance. Moreover, over the 5–10 year period of the Management Plan, it is possible that large adjustments may be required, due to changes to the protected area itself, to the surrounding area or to the staffing/financial situation of the managing organisation, or as a result of significant successes or failures. Therefore, many organisations use the Management Plan to identify the range of actions needed, and from which the more detailed and accurate operational plans (such as work plans) are produced (see Section 2.7).

Even where this approach is adopted, Management Plans can still serve as essential budget documents, since governments and donors are unlikely to fund actions not included in the plan. Moreover, a suite of Management Plans for all protected areas under the agency's responsibility provide the foundations for its business plan, with clear indications as to why the funding is required, management priorities and how resources will be allocated.

Agencies which operate on the basis described above include the Kwa Zulu Natal Nature Conservation Service and the Kenya Wildlife Service. Both use Management Plans as the starting point for the preparation of annual work plans. Any changes required to ensure that the work plan is relevant and up-to-date are considered and adjusted annually.

The second approach is adopted when countries or agencies decide to outline details of the financial and operational information as part of the Management Plan.

Where the second approach is adopted and this information is included it would be in the form of a *work plan* which should cover the activities to be carried out with an estimate of costs over the **entire** period of the Management Plan. This can be set out as a summary in spread sheet format. It should include: the timescale involved; the resources of staff and money required; the priority to be accorded to the work; and criteria for success and failure to be used to measure progress. Depending on how financial/resource planning is carried out in the organisation, it may be useful to split the work plan into two parts:

- repeated and on-going tasks (maintenance programme);
- developmental or capital projects, or "one off" actions.

Detailed **annual** *operational plans* for the protected area should also be prepared on a rolling basis. These should be linked to annual budgets and provide an accurate projection of the work to be carried out in a protected area each year derived from the Management Plan. As with the work plan, it may help to distinguish between repeated or on-going tasks, and developmental or capital projects. *Operational plans would not normally form part of the Management Plan but serve as a management tool setting out how it will be implemented.*

Some variations in presentation

There are several ways in which information relating to implementation can be grouped in the Management Plan or any supporting document:

By zone

If management zones have been identified, the actions, times and costs for the protected area may be grouped together thus:

- actions which are required for each zone;
- actions which are wide in their application, affecting more than one zone; and
- actions that extend outside the protected area.

By objective

In some cases, actions – along with associated timelines and costings – are grouped into 'management strategies' for each objective.

Division into projects

In other cases, management actions (sometimes called prescriptions) are broken down into units of work called "projects". This can facilitate implementation as each project can be clearly described, individually costed and timetabled. Documentation relating to the project can be used to guide members of staff, or contractors, charged with carrying out the work.

Within this approach, each project is assigned a **priority.** The priority order is used to guide an annual allocation of resources. One way to organise priorities is as follows:

- **Priority 1:** projects which need to be completed within a given year. These might include projects which are essential to safeguard key characteristics of the site, those that relate to legal implications of site tenure, and those that have implications under health and safety and public liability.

- **Priority 2:** projects which are important for routine management of the protected area. They should be completed in a given time period, but with an element of flexibility.

- **Priority 3:** projects which, though desirable, may only be undertaken when time or other resources are available following completion of projects under Priorities 1 and 2.

Step 12. Monitoring and review

The purpose of monitoring and review

When the Management Plan has been prepared and approved, and the operational plans are in place to guide its implementation, field staff are then able to put the plan into practice. With implementation under way, monitoring and review will provide the feedback loop. The purposes of this step are: to identify whether the plan is being implemented effectively and the objectives are being met; to learn from observation of the impacts of management; and to adapt the management actions accordingly. Where implementation runs into problems, monitoring and review can be used to re-deploy resources and effort to improve implementation.

The IUCN framework for assessing management effectiveness deals with the whole issue of monitoring and evaluation of protected area management and provides detailed guidance as to how a monitoring and evaluative process should be designed and implemented (Hockings *et al.*, 2000). It focuses on two aspects:

■ *the appropriateness of management systems and processes*: measured by assessing the management inputs required and the processes used; and

■ *the delivery of protected area objectives*: measured by identifying the outputs and outcomes of management.

Within this broad division, IUCN identifies six main elements of the management process which can be evaluated to identify the level and location of success or failure within the management cycle:

■ Where are we now? (context)

■ Where do we want to be? (planning)

■ What do we need? (input)

■ How do we go about it? (process)

■ What were the results? (outputs – i.e. the activities carried out or services provided)

■ What did we achieve? (outcomes – i.e. the actual achievements of management)

In terms of assessing management effectiveness, an evaluation of outcomes against objectives is the most relevant test. However, this may require significant monitoring effort in situations where little attention has been given to assessing outcomes in the past. Many objectives and management targets are not written specifically enough to suggest obvious outcomes which would indicate success. Furthermore, even where they are described clearly, our understanding of the underlying ecological processes is often an inadequate basis for claiming success. It is usually easier to conclude a measure has failed than to conclude it has succeeded.

Types of monitoring

In the past, many organisations have limited their monitoring to 'implementation monitoring' i.e. checking whether work has been carried out as specified in the plan. This is sometimes referred to as 'efficiency evaluation' and is a fairly straightforward task. For example, an annual report from the manager indicating activities carried out for the year will enable an evaluation of how much of the planned programme has been completed. This information will then be used to inform the review of projects and work programmes for the following year.

The problem is that this information does not tell the manager if the **objectives** are being achieved. It can tell if the manager has been busy – not whether he or she has been effective. So it provides little understanding of the outputs of management and still less about its outcomes: it is not an informative approach. What is needed is critical scrutiny of whether objectives are being achieved or whether they are the right ones for the site. In their absence, there are bound to be problems of 'accountability'. As Lipscombe explains:

"without it, managers have no evidence to support or refute the usefulness of the way they and their staff spend their day: they have no defence when called to be accountable to their bureaucratic or political masters or to the tax-paying public" (Lipscombe 1987).

However, accountability and assessment of the effectiveness of management are also difficult to achieve without the presence of specific and measurable objectives within the Management Plan itself, as already noted above.

In addition to the work by Hockings *et al.,* other examples of management evaluation programmes have developed to inform the management of protected areas. For example, the concept of 'Common Standards Monitoring' has been developed in the UK for nature conservation sites covered by statutory designations (for further explanation, see page 35). Parks Canada has a statutory requirement to protect park integrity and to report publicly on the extent to which this is being achieved.

Step 13. Decision to review and update the Management Plan

The final step in the planning process is to decide on either review or update of the Management Plan. In many cases, the plan will be time-limited by legislation, typically for five, seven or ten years. The decision to undertake a revision needs to be made in sufficient time to allow the new plan to be in place before the expiry of the old one. In cases of a complex plan with extensive public consultation process, it may be necessary to consider embarking on the review two years prior to the new plan coming into effect. In less complicated situations, the process should commence at least 12 months before the new plan takes effect.

An integral part of this final step is to ensure that feedback from the monitoring cycle is available to guide drafting of the new document. It may be appropriate to commission an evaluation study to collect monitoring information where this is not available, or to commission further studies to provide in-depth information on issues that have not been well covered by monitoring. The time needed for this work should be factored into the decision to update the Management Plan, so that it does not cause delay, and indeed the intent to undertake the evaluation should form part of the Management Plan itself.

There will be instances where an approved Management Plan has no defined expiry date. While legally the basic document may continue, it is unlikely that the management prescriptions will remain valid in perpetuity. Hence management agencies should accept the need to revise plans at appropriate intervals rather than try to work with out-of-date plans. It is recommended that Management Plans be reviewed at least every ten years.

5. Involving people

5.1 Why involve people

"In an age of ombudsmen, freedom of information and generally increased bureaucratic accountability of 'open government' – the time when decisions in park management could be made 'behind closed doors' with impunity is probably over" (Lipscombe 1987).

What was 'probably' true more than 15 years ago is undoubtedly the case now. Indeed it is now standard good practice to include people with an interest or a 'stake' in a protected area in the management planning process. These people include local communities, user groups, interested individuals, local government officials, representatives of NGOs, commercial interests, many other groups and – of course – the staff of the protected area itself. The inclusion of local communities has received specific emphasis and indeed the need for protected area management to have an 'outward focus' was one of the key recommendations of the IVth World Parks Congress held in Caracas in 1992.

Involving a wide range of people in the planning process can be time consuming. Moreover, consultation carries many risks: for example, it can "trap managers between the 'unrealistic' aspirations of some groups, 'rigid' legislation, 'distant' supervisors and the impossible demands of donors and pressure groups" (Scholte 2000). But the involvement of the various interests is essential if there is to be consensus around the aims of the Management Plan. Indeed, while including people in the planning process can present a challenge, this is far outweighed by the benefits – see Box 17.

Box 17. Benefits of involving people in management planning

- Increased **sense of 'ownership'**. Communities living in or near the protected area, visitors and other users of parks will feel a far greater commitment to park management objectives and practices if they have the opportunity to be involved in determining those ends and means.

- Greater **support** for the protection of the area. The success of a plan will depend on public and political support. It is essential to maintain regular communication with the public on decisions that affect them, and on the protection and use of the protected area.

- Greater public **involvement** in decision-making, helping people to be aware of [and to feel they can influence] changes in management direction.

- Links planning for conservation with planning for **development**. Not taking account of the needs of people in terms of economic and social development means a Management Plan has a poor chance of achieving its objectives.

- Provides a **mechanism for communication**, where views, concerns and opinions on management of the area can be shared between the managers and stakeholders. This can lead to the identification and resolution of problems and to a greater understanding and support for the protected area.

Protected area managers and organisations should be aware that not everyone will share their particular concerns about the protected area. There will be competing interests and values among the many people and communities affected by the protected area; if consensus is to be achieved on an acceptable course of future management, it will have to be built. The protected area staff will have to work hard to win the support and consent of these many interest groups. However good a Management Plan might be, it will not be accepted by the various interest groups without their involvement. Only through involvement can come ownership; only through ownership can come understanding and support.

5.2　Whom to involve

One of the fundamental questions to answer when embarking on a management planning process, is determining who the main 'stakeholders'are.

"There are many kinds of 'publics' and the first step is to identify who they are in your particular situation. Are they tourists, researchers, local hunters, farmers and fishermen, government officials, who?" (Thorsell 1995).

If local people live in or around the protected area, it will be important to involve them in the process. In relation to Category V protected areas, in which there is always a resident human population, IUCN has given detailed advice on the need for community participation at every stage in the planning and management process (Phillips, 2002). However, in every case it is important to identify what is 'local community'. Does this just apply to people who live within a particular distance of the area? How does one determine who should be involved? How should all legitimate interests be represented? The **Guidelines** in Box 18 ask a number of questions which are useful in identifying the key stakeholders for a protected area.

Box 18. Guidelines on identifying the key stakeholders

Key **individuals** with influence on the protected area might include:

- ministers and directors of other land and resource management authorities
- the leaders of the local community, action group or progress association
- adjacent landowners and home owners
- occupiers, including practising farmers and those renting property, or with licences or leases near the protected area
- business managers, the work force and their representatives involved in particular economic activities such as water supply, forestry, mineral extraction, fisheries and tourism
- protected area planners, managers and their work force
- representatives of those who organise or influence visitors to the area for leisure and recreational pursuits
- researchers with sites or projects in or near the area

The following **questions** may help identify the key stakeholders:

1. What are people's relationships with the area – how do they use and value it?
2. What are their various roles and responsibilities?
3. In what ways are they likely to be affected by any management initiative?
4. What is the current impact of their activities on the values of the protected area?

5.3 Types of involvement

Participation is the general term used to describe the involvement of groups and individuals in the decision-making process. There are many interpretations of this term and levels of participation possible, which are summarised below. Over time, management planning approaches have moved from very limited levels of participation to much more inclusive levels. However, the type of involvement chosen will depend very much on what the management agency hopes to achieve and how 'free' it is to involve others in the decision-making process. Many organisations are bound by their legislative or political mandate and unable to deviate from this. However, there will almost always be matters of detail and decisions on 'how' this mandate is to be met that could and should allow scope for participation with stakeholders.

Lipscombe (1987) advises:

"It is possible to find out what the public wants. However, it is an expensive and difficult process – in which one is never really certain of the truth. Full participation in planning should therefore never be taken on lightly. Where there are known to be conflicts of views it is likely to be worthwhile, it will bring to light matters of importance which the planner might otherwise miss. The most important aspect may simply be that people feel they have had a genuine opportunity to present their views – which have been seriously considered."

Levels of participation have been defined as follows:

Informing. This is the lowest level of participation. Groups and individuals receive information about proposed actions but have no opportunities to change them. The purpose of the information is usually to persuade others to the project leader's point of view. Communication is one way and represents a 'top-down' approach to decision-making in conservation.

Consulting. This is one step up from informing. Local communities, other key stakeholders and organisations receive information about a project or plan and their views are sought. The views of those consulted are usually taken account of, but not necessarily acted upon, when the final plan is drawn up, acknowledged or considered.

Deciding together. This occurs when those affected by an issue are invited to learn about it, discuss it and become part of the final decision-making process. Although they share in the process, those initiating the discussion usually set boundaries on how much influence the other stakeholders have in the final discussion.

Acting together is when there is both a shared decision-making process, and shared responsibility for implementing decisions.

Supporting independent community interests is the highest level of participation. Communities become responsible for setting their own agendas and implementing the decisions which they take. The role of experts and other agents or investors is to support the community with information and expertise and perhaps resources to help them take informed decisions. This represents a completely 'bottom-up' approach to conservation.

57

5.4 Consultation

There are several **Guidelines** which should be followed when involving people in the planning process, see Box 19.

Box 19. **Guidelines** on consultation

Involve people early: the earlier people are involved, the more opportunity they have to influence the outcomes. Desirably this includes the initial scoping exercise as planning starts.

Communicate: this should be two-way – the opinions of others are listened to, valued and a shared meaning is sought. A result of communication is improved knowledge of an issue and often convergence of opinion about it. Where disagreement exists the reasons for this will be known.

Provide information and education: providing information and education in appropriate forms helps people make decisions based on a sound understanding of the issues involved.

Allow adequate time: It is important to give sufficient time at the start to build relationships, understand and explore the issues, agree on, and collect, the data that people need, communicate regularly and exchange information and ideas and consider possible solutions and their implications.

Build in flexibility: plans need to be able to evolve as people's understanding of a situation evolves and as more information becomes available. Periodic reviews should be built in.

In addition to these guidelines, experience indicates the importance of providing **appropriate incentives** for local communities around protected areas to get involved in planning and management. For example, in a study of management planning in Indonesian coastal protected areas, it was found that unless coastal communities perceive real improvements to their socio-economic conditions there is no incentive to participate in marine protected area planning and management (Alder *et al.*, 1994). IUCN Pakistan also stress the importance of helping people to meet their development needs, before expecting them to participate in and **support** protected area management:

"Local peoples may not have viable options for supporting protected area management until they achieve higher productivity in their core economic activities and meet their basic needs."

"The desire for public and local involvement in protected area planning must be reinforced even further by providing direct economic benefits to local communities from protected areas projects. People must have a stake in the outcome, and although it need not always be an economic benefit, such benefits are often desirable in poor rural communities. [e.g. conservation through use.]" (IUCN Pakistan, 1984).

If stakeholders are to play a full role, they need to know who the decision-makers are and how the process of protected area management works. Local people should be encouraged to form interest groups; these should be assisted with **training and development** about the management planning process, and helped to develop their communication and negotiating skills. This will enable stakeholders to be better informed, more effective in the initial planning stages, more articulate about their concerns and desired outcomes for the planning process, better placed to participate in appropriate community development programmes, and more able to understand and accept decisions they might not agree with.

Local staff should not be forgotten in capacity building. Often they will pay a key role in communicating with local stakeholders, having local language skills and being knowledgeable about community traditions and concerns. It follows that the selection and training of local protected area staff are critical in relation to community involvement, and that skills in areas such as community consultation need to be developed and maintained

Few local people's views are consistent over time. As local communities change and adopt different views and priorities, so planners may have to revise their work. Planners need a close and sound working relationship with local communities, whilst maintaining their responsiveness to other factors relevant to this work.

5.5 Methods

"Generally, local communities are not used to being consulted and some may have difficulty in following even the clearest and most readable of documents. In many parts of the world, indeed, poor levels of literacy or the use of indigenous languages will require other approaches to consultation. The onus is on the agency to reach out to the community, but at the same time it will need to use its judgement as to how representative stakeholder groups really are" (Phillips, 2000).

Many methods can be used to involve people in the planning process. The following list of methods comes from the New South Wales National Parks and Wildlife Service. It is apparent that the methods in this list fall mostly into the categories of 'informing', 'consulting' and 'deciding together':

- press releases/advertisements inviting submissions
- radio/TV appearances to discuss planning issues
- publication of specialised pre-planning pamphlets/brochures which provide detailed discussion on specific issues
- publication of draft plans of management
- open forum public meetings to present and discuss planning documents
- pre-arranged meetings of special interest groups brought together to resolve conflicting requirements
- consultations between planners and individuals/organisations
- analysis of written public submissions by agencies and third parties
- referral of public submissions to external advisory groups e.g. consultative committees comprising community leaders/representatives
- formal involvement of independent statutory advisory committees in assessing plans and public submissions
- input through political processes, particularly in regard to more difficult issues

In other places less conventional techniques can be used. For example, as well as seminars and informal discussions, there are 'village drama', school plays and 'road shows' – whatever it takes to get people involved. Local elders, head teachers and other community leaders will advise the agency on the most appropriate way to engage the public.

Four examples of the practical application of public participation are given below in Boxes 20–23, showing the range of possible methods and how they can be applied in practice.

Box 20.   Public participation in Huascaran World Heritage Site, Peru

The process used here was very 'participative' and could be classified as 'deciding together', with people involved throughout the process and actively contributing to the decision-making. It consisted of six main steps:

1. *Presentation of a proposal for a Management Plan by letter.* This was distributed to rural and urban populations and to institutions in a nearby city.

2. *Discussions with users of the park* (including local communities and electricity/mining interests).

3. *Identification of basic problems.* For example, the need to draw up grazing agreements with communities, and the lack of agreed process for selecting projects for implementation in the park.

4. *Circulation of a survey* (based on the problems identified in 3.). This was distributed in rural and urban areas. Collection boxes were provided and radio announcements explained the aims of the survey and the importance of public participation. This survey identified a need for more and better information on the objectives of the Management Plan. It also indicated that rural communities possessed a sound practical understanding of environmental and conservation issues and that they were well disposed to reaching agreements with park authorities if real benefits would accrue to them as a result. This reassured planning staff – and speeded up the process.

5. *Organised inter-institutional working teams to analyse survey results.* These analysed the opinions of interest groups and staff and provided the basis of a first draft plan.

6. *Community workshops.* Twelve workshops were organised to inform local communities of the objectives of the Management Plan and to seek input from them. There were two parts to each workshop
   - discussion of serious park problems (using techniques such as role playing to convey some key ideas at public meetings); and
   - presentation of the proposed plan.

Comments were then used to re-formulate original proposals, including zoning.

Source: Angeles (1992).

Box 21.   Public participation in Fitzgerald River NP, Australia

A combination of the following techniques was used in the preparation of the plan, and to inform people, seek their views and involve them in direct decision-making:
   - advisory committees (members were nominated who had affiliations with one or more community groups);
   - circulation of leaflets (location; explanation that the Management Plan was being prepared; and an invitation to people to write regarding any issues of concern and of management problems);
   - issues workshops – these were held early in the planning process to identify demands and expectations of communities;
   - visitor questionnaires; and
   - meetings and forums.

Sources: Smith and Moore (1990) in Gulez (1992); Watson and Sanders (1997).

Box 22. Public participation in Riding Mountain Management Plan, Canada

Three steps were used in this public participation exercise:

1. Planning staff met with public many times to present and discuss all available information on the park and its resources; public audiences submitted their opinions/comments/suggestions for park development and for alternative planning concepts.

2. Three alternative park planning concepts were prepared and presented for public review and comment.

3. Final step – this had as its objective to work together (via public meetings) to select the best conceptual ideas as an approach to the eventual Management Plan.

Box 23. Public participation in Peak District National Park, England

A three stage 'consultative' approach was used to seek views before final decisions were made by the managing organisation:

1. Options for the different park activities (conservation, recreation, transportation etc.) were taken into account and different options for each management activity were then presented to the public for comment.

2. General strategies for the park were then set out for comment.

3. In the light of public comments, a preferred strategy was chosen by the national park authority.

5.6 Towards community based planning

Though not yet commonly adopted, some protected area authorities and stakeholders share the responsibility for decisions made. Some go even further and recognise that communities can become responsible for setting their own agendas and implementing the decisions that they take. This process is sometimes called 'community based planning', 'collaborative planning' or 'co-management'. Two examples are provided here (Boxes 24 and 25) to illustrate how this most challenging of approaches can work. Co-management fulfils many of the demands from stakeholders for more responsibility for decision-making, but it also places the onus on them to share responsibility for delivering the agreed plan.

Box 24. Public Participation in Central Karakoram National Park and World Heritage Site, Pakistan

In 1994, a workshop was held to try to develop a community based planning process for this World Heritage site. The participants of this workshop (including park officials, NGOs and local community representatives) wanted the planning process to be set in a broader context of sustainable development of the local area, and to include full involvement of local people in decision-making.

The workshop adapted a generic management planning process to meet the needs of the area, the characteristics of its rural communities and social and economic issues. The result was a set of guidelines for customising the planning process:

1. Undertake planning activities in the context of a district level sustainable development strategy. This will broaden the mandate, take more time and cost more money – but the end result may benefit more people.

2. Begin the process by forming a steering committee for the whole programme, which focuses on appropriate sustainable development activities in the park and surrounding area. Allow this body to **self-define** its planning priorities – to define the tasks and hire the technical team.

3. Ensure that legitimate interests are represented on the steering committee, e.g. village representatives, union councils, religious authorities and adventure travel companies.

4. Create a series of valley-specific subgroups to consider in detail the needs of each valley. While there may be many issues in common, there are cultural differences, environmental variations, political differences and potentially different solutions available for each subgroup.

5. Establish subgroups to work on different themes inside and outside the park, e.g. tools for tourism management and infrastructure improvement.

6. Select the technical support team chosen, as far as possible, from **local** professionals. Provide internships and training opportunities wherever possible. Capacity development within the community should be a principal objective throughout the planning and development exercise.

7. Work through and strengthen existing councils and village structures/organisations. This may require training for technical planning subjects – but it will pay long-term dividends.

8. Base the planning process *in* the area. Regional/national staff should be expected to travel into the area.

9. Provide adequate resources to facilitate participation and involvement by local representatives (e.g. travel expenses). The value of the participation should be publicly acknowledged.

10. Involve the private sector to the fullest extent possible, including local, national and international eco-tourism and adventure travel companies.

11. Market the process. Once there is consensus on the basic tenets of the regional management and park management objectives, make sure the travel industry, international organisations and NGOs understand and become supportive.

12. Use the planning process to formulate some implementation activities (e.g. site rehabilitation).

13. Use the planning process to help train wildlife wardens, park rangers and protected area managers from other parts of the country.

Source: IUCN Pakistan (1994).

Box 25. Public participation in Bwindi Impenetrable Forest, Uganda

In this case study, the authors document a 'collaborative management' process. This is defined as "the process of collaboration between local communities and state agencies over the use and management of natural resources and other assets, either state or privately owned, through a process of negotiation which includes all stakeholders, recognizes the contribution of each and results in mutually acceptable and adaptable agreement".

It was carried out as follows:

1. Resource use of the forest by local people was discussed with community members during the writing of the Management Plan for Bwindi in 1993–94;

2. Small planning teams and project staff were established to produce the plan. The teams chose the basic plan format and designed a programme of planning workshops involving community participation; and

3. Key planning decisions were made first at the local level and then at a national level. At Bwindi, workshop approaches taken from other plans were adapted and small groups worked on sections of the plan, both making the decisions and drafting the text.

Although a difficult and time consuming exercise, it was found that this process facilitated genuine and meaningful community participation in protected area management and significantly enhanced park interactions with the communities and administration. Wild and Mutebi cite its benefits to include:

1. Solutions to urgent conflicts were discussed and action plans produced;

2. Consensus planning between all major stakeholders was initiated;

3. A sense of ownership was promoted among park staff for the planning process;

4. Community leaders became convinced that park designation could have benefits;

5. A planning context was established for parish level negotiations concerning resource use and management;

6. Mechanisms were established for community involvement in park management; and

7. Significant local knowledge was documented and utilised.

In this approach, the process of planning was equally, if not more important than the plan document itself, with far reaching and positive spin-offs:

> *"It contrasted with the earlier Uganda National Park Plans, produced by an external expert and based on consultations mostly with park staff. The final output of participatory planning was less polished and needed refining. In the longer term, the involvement of community members had unexpected and positive implications. Some individuals went on to represent the community on local and national conservation bodies and became strong advocates for conservation within their own communities".*

Source: Wild and Mutebi (1997).

6. The international dimension to management planning

In many cases there is an international dimension to management planning. This adds a 'gloss' to the process described in the foregoing Chapters, but does not fundamentally change the process. The following additional guidance is offered in relation to World Heritage Areas, Ramsar sites, UNESCO Biosphere Reserves, regional agreements and transboundary arrangements.

6.1 The management of World Heritage sites[1]

The purpose of management of a World Heritage property is to ensure the protection of its "outstanding universal value" for the benefit of the present generation, and its transmission unimpaired to future generations.

World Heritage properties may sustain a variety of actual or proposed uses. Some uses may be essential to the maintenance of a property, for example traditional uses by indigenous peoples. Furthermore, any uses should be ecologically and culturally sustainable. For some properties, human use would not be appropriate.

Each property should have an appropriate Management Plan or other documented management system. The management system should demonstrate effective administrative, contractual, and/or traditional management mechanisms, protection systems and/or planning controls. An explanation of how these management mechanisms, protection systems and planning controls operate, should also be provided by the State Party in the nomination. In some circumstances, a Management Plan or other management system may not be in place at the time when a site is nominated for the consideration of the World Heritage Committee. The State Party concerned should then indicate when such a Management Plan or system would be put in place, and how it proposes to mobilise the resources required for its preparation and implementation.

Effective management planning involves a cycle of long-term and day-to-day actions to protect, conserve and present the World Heritage property. Common elements of the recommended management approach for World Heritage sites include:

- a cycle of planning, implementation, monitoring, evaluation and feedback;
- planning based on a thorough understanding of the property;
- the full involvement of partners and stakeholders;
- capacity-building for all involved in the planning process; and
- application of the Precautionary Principle.

Close attention should be given to the development of management planning approaches, designed according to the capacity of the World Heritage property and its

---

[1] *See also* the Operational Guidelines for the Implementation of the World Heritage Convention, UNESCO (2002). A new version of this is expected to be published during 2003.

cultural and natural context. Approaches may vary according to different cultural perspectives, the type of property, resources available and other factors. They may incorporate traditional practices, existing urban or regional planning instruments, and other planning control mechanisms, both formal and informal depending on the circumstances.

An accountable, transparent system showing how a property is to be monitored is essential. The management approach should also include a mechanism for Periodic Reporting on a six year cycle as an integral part of the planning effort.

6.2 Ramsar Sites[2]

Wetlands are dynamic areas, open to influence from natural and human factors. In order to maintain their biological diversity and productivity and to allow wise use of their resources by human beings, some kind of overall agreement is needed between the various owners, occupiers and interested parties. The management planning process provides this overall agreement.

When developing management planning, which will be applied to all wetlands and not just to reserves, the following considerations should be taken into account:

■ Management planning is a way of thinking which involves recording, evaluating and planning. It is a process subject to constant review and revision. Management Plans should, therefore, be flexible, dynamic documents.

■ It is essential to emphasise that – in essence – the process described below is very simple. It involves three basic actions: describing, defining objectives, and taking any necessary action. Preparation of an elaborate plan must never be an excuse for inaction or delay. It will be useful to produce a very brief executive summary for decision-makers in order to allow decisions of principle and funding to be taken rapidly.

■ Review of the plan may lead to revision of the site description and objectives (particularly the operational objectives).

The format of the Management Plan for Ramsar sites, as is reflected in these guidelines, should comprise the following elements:

Preamble
1. Description
2. Evaluation and objectives *(i.e. what to do)*
    2.1 Evaluation
    2.2 Long-term objectives
    2.3 Factors influencing achievement of long-term objectives
    2.4 Operational objectives

3. Action plan/prescriptions *(i.e. how to do it)*
    3.1 Work plan
    3.2 Projects
    3.3 Work programmes
    3.4 Annual review
    3.5 Major review

---

[2] Extracted from Ramsar Handbooks for the Wise Use of Wetlands, No. 8 *Frameworks for Managing Wetlands of International Importance and Other Wetlands*.

For further details in relation to Ramsar management planning, the reader is referred to the Ramsar handbook.

6.3 UNESCO Biosphere Reserves

Biosphere Reserves have no fixed format to be adhered to in drafting Management Plans. By their nature, Biosphere Reserves will nearly always include a combination of public and privately owned lands. Accordingly the development of management prescriptions for inclusion in a Management Plan may not be feasible except at the broadest level. That is not to say that different components may not have Management Plans developed for them. Indeed it is frequently the case that core protected areas have detailed Management Plans while the remaining areas adhere to less prescriptive but widely cast objectives, for example in land use policies. Other objectives for buffer and transition zones may relate to sustainable practices, for example to promote the production of "organically grown" fruit produce, or operate sound water use practices.

Broad consultation in the development of relevant policies and practices is vital in the development of Management Plans for Biosphere Reserves. Unless there is such participation in their development and adoption, it is unlikely that the desired framework will be accepted or adhered to, and the objectives met. Consultative management planning is accordingly an essential requirement for Biosphere Reserves.

6.4 Protected areas subject to international or regional agreements

Protected areas proclaimed within a national system may also be subject to international or regional agreements, some of which – such as Natura 2000 in Europe – are very exacting in their management requirements. Other agreements, such as those made under the auspices of the UNEP Regional Seas Programme, the South Pacific Regional Environment Programme or the ASEAN agreement are more discretionary, but these too may influence the content of the policies in the Management Plan. It is obvious therefore that planners need to be aware of any specific requirements of such agreements.

6.5 Transboundary arrangements

Many protected areas share national or provincial boundaries and adjoin other protected areas across the boundary. IUCN reported 666 such complexes in 1997 (Zbicz, D. in Sandwith *et al.*, 2001). It is obvious that poor planning can result in incompatible activities in areas on either side of the boundary. For example, the zoning of a wilderness area on one side of a boundary could be compromised by infrastructure development on the other. Coordinated planning can reduce this risk, and ensure that the partners develop an appreciation of their relative biophysical, political, social and economic contexts. Therefore, IUCN promotes closer co-operation between neighbouring administrations in such situations (see Sandwith *et al.*, 2001).

Coordinated planning is indeed essential if the purposes of the protected areas involved are to be translated into effective programmes for management and development. Integrated planning ensures that all interests in neighbouring countries or provinces should be involved and that the consequences of decisions for sectoral programmes are fully evaluated. The process of planning, if handled in a participatory manner, can promote commitment and empowerment among stakeholders on both sides of the boundary, as well as capacity building where there would otherwise be unequal experience or skill.

Ideally Management Plans should be prepared jointly to ensure consistency of planning and management. Management Plans should be based upon the same vision and objectives, and implemented through action plans that are consistent with each country's managing procedures.

7. Abbreviated planning approaches

If a full Management Plan is not required, or cannot be prepared within the time and resources available, an abbreviated form of the management planning process can still be carried out, resulting in an interim plan. It is thus a 'stop-gap' measure intended to guide managers on appropriate and acceptable activity until such time as a full plan can be prepared.

Such guidance can be as simple as a statement of the values to be protected and the most basic actions needed to maintain those values. However a rather more useful approach is the preparation of a broader document that includes a set of policies that address specific management issues, types of use and principles of infrastructure development. In this latter case, the process:

- identifies the key features and management objectives;
- may include a management zoning scheme that identifies what can and cannot be done with specific emphasis on development and use;
- briefly assesses the environmental issues; and
- provides an interim implementation plan.

In Central America, a slightly different approach has been taken to providing management guidance in the absence of a Management Plan. Some protected area organisations have prepared detailed operational plans (short-term, and usually annual) for the entire system of protected areas, and for all central office technical and administrative departments of some management agencies. These have then been combined to produce an overall operational plan for the whole organisation. In most cases, several rounds of such planning have taken place, with the plans implemented and initial evaluations completed. The results to date are encouraging. At the strategic level, they appear to have led to significantly improved management of the organisation concerned, its technical and administrative departments; at the level of individual protected areas, it has helped to establish priorities and provide an important level of protection.

Recent experience in Latin America also suggests the adoption of a simplified form of Management Plan, though in fact it requires many of the same elements recommended in these Guidelines. It suggests that Management Plans should contain:

- A "descriptive compendium" (geographical, biophysical, social and economic information related to the protected area);
- A compendium of laws, norms and agreements, as a basis for any legal matters related to the protected area;
- A strategic plan, prioritising the management activities, answering in broad terms the questions what to do, where and how? and
- A zoning plan, regulating the use of the area and its resources, defining with precision where things can be done and how (Amend *et al.*, 2003).

Annex: Roles, responsibilities and skills

The planning team

As noted earlier, (section 4.2, Step 1) a planning team should be established to guide the preparation of the plan at the outset of the process. The team's role will be to understand and describe the purposes of the park and to formulate guidelines for the protection, use, development and interpretation of its resources.

To be successful, the planning team should:

1. be interdisciplinary and contain experts with different professional backgrounds, e.g. ecologists, landscape architects, park planners, social scientists (such as sociologists and anthropologists), resource managers, engineers and technical experts. The expertise required will depend on the circumstances of the protected area, its socio-economic conditions, and the management issues and prescriptions to be developed;

2. involve the management and staff from the protected area in question. As Parr points out:

    "it is very largely these individuals who will implement the plan. Equally important, they probably have the best perception of what really can be achieved within the protected area, with any given budget, over a period of time" (Parr 1998);

3. include other staff from within the organisation (district, regional or Head Office staff) to provide guidance on policy, regional and national context;

4. possess insight and imagination. Its members should have the ability to think creatively and solve problems. Team members should also possess the skills needed to communicate their ideas and values to each other and to external interests:

    "The process of planning is people oriented. The planning process deals with what people, both inside and outside the park management organisation, want done and how they think it should be achieved. Planning is a process for structuring thinking about these issues and communicating them, either in writing or some other form.

    Skills in communication, be it in writing or in handling negotiations in large and small meetings are now indispensable from the list of skills that should be available on any park management planning team. Increasingly planning is about being able to handle people rather than pieces of paper" (Lipscombe 1987);

5. include local people on the team where feasible and appropriate. They will be able to contribute knowledge of local conditions and their involvement should encourage the acceptance of the plan by local communities. If they are not directly

involved in the planning team itself, they should certainly be involved in the preparatory process and subsequent steps.

The project manager, the planner and the author

Three key responsibilities must be assigned to members of the planning team:

1. Someone to co-ordinate and organise production of the plan, i.e. a project manager;

2. Someone to advise on the planning process, the approach to be taken, the methods to be used, i.e. a planner/planning adviser;

3. Someone to draft the plan, or to have editorial control if different sections are contributed by different people, i.e. an author/editor.

These roles can be filled by the same person, or by different people. Commonly a professional planner will sit on a planning team and fulfil the roles of planning adviser and author. A different member of staff may then act as project manager. Alternatively, the protected area manager can act as author of the plan, with assistance from the planner. The planner will probably be from a regional or national office of the organisation. This approach is one favoured by many who feel that full involvement by the manager(s) will improve the prospects for implementation (Alexander 1995; Sandwith 1997). The presence of the regional/HQ planner as adviser encourages a consistent approach across all areas within the remit of the organisation and provides an element of 'quality control' and consistency of approach for the managing authority.

These three roles, and the skills required, are outlined below:

Project manager

The primary responsibility of the project manager is to ensure that the plan is prepared to schedule and budget. This will involve identification of the tasks involved, preparation of a work plan, allocation of responsibilities, ensuring deadlines are met etc.

The ideal qualities of a project manager have been defined by Scott:

"an habitual broad perspective style of thinking; an orderly mind which can integrate a large number of factors into a harmonious whole; an ability to communicate lucidly and concisely; an ability to get things done quickly; an ability to resolve conflict; an ability to run a meeting effectively since meetings will be the principal communications and decision-making forum" (Scott in Kelleher and Kenchington 1991).

A series of project management "lessons" which can usefully be applied to the process of management planning are summarised in Box 25 below.

Box 25. Lessons from project management

Participants function best when they have a broad understanding of the total picture. Time spent in group discussion of the problems and discussions will help achieve this broad understanding and build a team:

- the number of key participants must be kept to a realistic minimum and their quality to a maximum;
- the participants should be selected carefully and rationally after a detailed preliminary analysis of the protected areas and the skills required;
- the individual(s) who will eventually manage the PA system or sites should be key members of the team;
- the project manager's function is that of integrator, coordinator, communications centre, tactician and consensus builder;
- the project should be organised in an organic/adaptive fashion. All aspects should be orchestrated so that decisions follow an orderly progress, and maximum flexibility is retained;
- scheduling should concentrate on the broad aspects of key project elements rather than getting bogged down in detail; and
- cost control should rely on advance development of remedial tactics to stay within budget.

Source: Kelleher (1999).

Planner/Planning adviser

The role of the planner within the team is primarily one of co-ordinator, communicator and facilitator. "It is his [or her] responsibility to pull together a diversity of opinion and factual data to create a whole out of myriad parts" (Eidsvik 1977). The planner is also there to contribute a knowledge of the planning process itself and to "provide the design skills for formulating and evaluating the possible policy alternative and assist in the choice of the best solution" (Forster 1973). Often the planner is also the collector, organiser and processor of technical information (Driver 1970).

The planner is not normally an expert in individual technical subjects and as such is not a direct decision-maker when it comes to deciding policy or management direction. His or her role is to facilitate the decision-making process. However, planners often do make direct decisions about the information that is included in the process and how it is used, and can therefore have an influence over the decisions made (Driver 1970). The planner must be aware of this responsibility and have integrity and objectivity when sorting and presenting information to the rest of the team.

The planner should be able to think systematically. He or she should have the ability to ask the right questions, weigh the evidence contributed by the scientific experts on the team and work with them to determine management alternatives and the relative long-term effects on values held by various interests (Forster 1973). Writing about planning for National Parks in North America in the 1970s (where the focus was on landscape preservation and the provision of recreational opportunities), Forster also listed these as desirable attributes: "awareness and aesthetic appreciation of the landscape and of the values and functions of environmental form", and "an understanding for the interpretation of human needs and for the construction of facilities associated with the context of park values and ecological principles"(Forster 1973).

Perhaps the most important skills a planner can have are the ability to think clearly, to analyse and to be creative in problem solving. Management planning is a mixture of analysis and creativity, and the planner has to be skilled in both areas:

"The evaluation process is an analytical process in which the planner must critically assess the data available. He [/she] must discover weaknesses as well as strengths. To do this he [/she] must pull things apart and examine the pieces. The creative portion of the planning process begins with problem definition"
(Eidsvik 1977).

When the planner is also acting as the author of the plan, the ability to think and communicate clearly becomes even more important:

"Perhaps the planning process can best be explained as a series of subconscious conversations which the planner has with himself – the question posed, the factors weighed, and then the recorded conclusion. The more lucid the thinking, the more coherent the powers of idea communication....the better the plan" (Simonds 1961 (in Eidsvik 1977)).

"Irrespective of the processes and parties involved in the preparation of a [conservation] plan, it is finally the practitioner who must shape and take responsibility for its contents. If approached without a preconceived agenda, evolved with skill, acquired contextual knowledge and integrity, and drafted with precision and clarity, the plan will make a positive contribution to the future of the place" (Kerr 1996).

Author

The ability to communicate in writing is the most important skill the author or editor of the plan must possess. Writing a Management Plan is a difficult task that requires considerable skill – something that should not be underestimated when assigning this responsibility within a planning team. For this reason, some organisations provide 'set text' (where possible) for certain sections of plans or detailed guidance on the required content and style of each section. The Kwa Zulu Natal Nature Conservation Service provides assistance in this way, with detailed guidance in both a planning manual and a computer template for the Management Plan (Sandwith 2000 pers. com.). This can be very helpful to the authors, who are often park managers and may not have much experience in drafting complex documents.

References

Alder, J., Sloan, N.A. and Uktolseya, H. (1994). A comparison of management planning and implementation in three Indonesian protected areas. *Ocean and Coastal Management* **24**.

Alexander, M. (1996). *A guide for the production of Management Plans for nature reserves and protected areas*. Countryside Council for Wales, Bangor, UK.

Alexander, M. (1995). Management planning in Relation to Protected Areas. *PARKS* **8(1)**.

Alexander, M. and Rowell,T.A. (1999). Recent Developments in Management Planning and Monitoring on Protected Sites in the UK. *PARKS* **9(2)**.

Amend, S., Giraldo, A., Oltermari, J., Sánchez, R., Valarezo, V. and Yerena, E. (2000). *Management Plans: Concepts and Proposals*. IUCN, San José, Costa Rica and Quito, Ecuador [in English and Spanish].

Angeles, M.T. (1992). Public Involvement in Huascaran World Heritage Site, Peru. *PARKS* **3(3)**.

Anon. (a) (undated). Developing a Management Plan. Unpublished paper, IUCN.

Anon. (b) (undated). Plans of Management: procedures for the development of Plans of Management for Protected Areas. Draft report for consideration of CONCOM Working Group on Management of National Parks (Australia) (unpublished).

ANZECC Working Group on National Parks and Protected Areas (2000). *Best Practice in Protected Area Management Planning*.

Beltrán, J. (ed). *Indigenous and Traditional Peoples and Protected Areas: Principles, guidelines and case studies*. IUCN, Gland, Switzerland and Cambridge, UK.

Budowski, G. and Macfarland, C. (1982). Keynote address: The Neotropical Realm. In McNeely and Miller (1982). *National Parks, Conservation and development. Proceedings of the World Congress on National Parks and Protected Areas*. Smithsonian Institution Press, Washington DC, USA.

Chettamart, S. (1985). Preparing a Management Plan for Khao Yai Park: the process involved and the lessons learned. In Thorsell, J (ed). *Conserving Asia's Natural Heritage*. IUCN, Gland, Switzerland.

Child, G. (1994). An Evaluation of the Tanzania National Parks Management Planning Project (IUCN, Gland Switzerland, unpublished).

Claridge, G. (1999). Protected Area Management Planning. *Tiger Paper* **26(2)**:15–17.

Clarke, J.E. (2000). Protected Area Management Planning. *Oryx* **34(2)**:85–89.

Clarke, J.E. (1997). *Manual for Protected Area Management Planning version 2.1*. Punjab Wildlife Research Institute/Punjab Wildlife and Parks Department.

Clarke, P. (1999). Park Management Planning in Africa – Opinion. *Oryx* **33(4)**.

Clarke, R. and Mount, D. (1998). *Management Plans and Planning: a guide*. Countryside Commission, Cheltenham, UK.

Cole, D.N. and Stankey, G.H. (1997). Historical development of Limits of Acceptable Change: conceptual clarifications and possible extensions. In *Proceedings: Limits of Acceptable Change and Related Planning processes: Progress and Future Directions.General Technical Report.* US Department of Agriculture Forest Service.

Colt, A.B. (1994). The First Step in Comparatively Evaluating Implementation of an Integrated Estuarine Management Plan. *Ocean and Coastal Management* **24**.

Countryside Commission (1997). *National Park Management Plans Guidance.* Countryside Commission, Cheltenham, UK.

Countryside Commission for Scotland (1989). *Management Plans for Country Parks: a guide to their preparation.* Countryside Commission for Scotland, Perth, UK.

Cullen, P. (1999). The Turbulent Boundary Beween Water Science and Management. *Freshwater Biology* **24**:201–209.

Davey, A.G. (1998). *National System Planning for Protected Areas.* Best Practice Protected Area Guidelines Series No. 1. IUCN, Gland, Switzerland and Cambridge, UK.

Davey, A. (1985). Issues in Management Planning for Australia's Alpine Areas: examples from the ACT's Namadgi National Park. Paper presented at a conference on Australia's alpine areas: management for conservation (unpublished).

Driver, B.L. (1970). *Some thoughts on Planning, the planning process and related decision processes.* (Publisher not known).

Eagles, P.F.J. (1984). *The Planning and Management of Environmentally Sensitive Areas.* Longman Group Limited, London, UK.

Eagles, P.F.J., Mccool S.F., Haynes, C.D. (2002). *Sustainable Tourism in Protected Areas: Guidelines for Planning and Management.* Best Practice Protected Area Guidelines Series No. 8. IUCN, Gland, Switzerland and Cambridge, UK.

EC/IUCN (1999). *Parks for Biodiversity: policy guidance based on experience in ACP countries.* IUCN, Cambridge, UK.

Eidsvik, H.K. (1977). The Park Planning Process. *PARKS* **2(3):** 8–12.

Eurosite (1999). *Toolkit: Management Planning.* Eurosite, Lille, France.

Forster, R.R. (1973). *Planning for Man and Nature in National Parks: reconciling perpetuation and use.* IUCN, Morges, Switzerland.

Glick, D. (1984). Management Planning in the Platano River Biosphere Reserve, Honduras. In *Conservation, Science and Society. Proceedings of the First Biosphere Reserves Congress, Minsk, USSR 1983.* UNESCO/UNEP.

Grobler, J.H. (1984). Management Planning: the Natal Parks Board (RSA) Approach. *PARKS* **9(1).**

Gunderson, L.H., Holling, C.S. and Light, S.S. (eds). 1995. *Barriers and Bridges to Renewal of Ecosystems and Institutions.* Columbia University Press, New York, USA.

Hockings, M. (1996). Integrating Planning and Evaluation: designing an evaluation strategy for management of the Fraser Island World Heritage Area. In *Papers and Proceedings of World Heritage Managers Workshop 1996.* Wet Tropics Management Authority, Canberra, Australia.

Harmon, D. (ed.) 1994. *Co-ordinating Research and Management to Enhance Protected Areas.* IUCN, Gland, Switzerland and Cambridge, UK.

Hockings, M. (1998). Evaluating Management of Protected Areas: Integrating Planning and Evaluation. *Environmental Management* **22(3)**.

Hockings, M., Stolton, S. and Dudley, N. (2000). *Evaluating Effectiveness: A Framework for Assessing the Management of Protected Areas.* IUCN, Gland, Switzerland and Cambridge, UK.

Howard, A.H. and Francis, J.J. (1992). National Park Management in Australia: the New South Wales Approach. Paper presented at the IVth World Congress on National Parks, Caracas (unpublished).

Idle, E.T. (1980). *Management Plans for Nature Conservation.* NCC Discussion Paper, Nature Conservancy Council, Edinburgh, UK.

IUCN (2000a). *Financing Protected Areas: Guidelines for Protected Area Managers.* IUCN, Gland, Switzerland and Cambridge, UK.

IUCN (2000b). Towards Sustainable Management of Sahelian Floodplains (leaflet). IUCN, Africa.

IUCN (1994). *Guidelines for Protected Area Management Categories.* IUCN, Gland, Switzerland and Cambridge, UK.

IUCN (1992). *Caracas Action Plan.* IUCN, Gland, Switzerland.

IUCN Pakistan Programme (1994). *Proceedings of Karakoram Workshop.* IUCN, Gland, Switzerland.

Jensen, M.O. (1989). Critical Elements of General Management Plans for National Parks. *International Workshop on the Management Planning of Khunjerab National Park. Proceedings*, IUCN, Gland, Switzerland.

Kelleher, G. (1999). *Guidelines for Marine Protected Areas.* IUCN, Gland, Switzerland and Cambridge, UK.

Kelleher, G. and Kenchington, R. (1991). *Guidelines for Establishing Marine Protected Areas.* IUCN, Gland, Switzerland and Cambridge, UK.

Kenya Wildlife Service (1990). *A policy framework and development programme 1991–96.* Annex 4: National Park and Reserve Planning (prepared by J.E. Clarke). Kenya Wildlife Service.

Kerr, J.S. (1996). *The Conservation Plan: a guide to the preparation of conservation plans for places of European cultural significance.* The National Trust, Australia.

Linn, R.M. (1977). Introduction to Master Planning. *PARKS* **1(1)**.

Lipscombe, N.R. (1987). *Park Management Planning: A guide to the writing of Management Plans.* Johnstone Centres of Parks and Recreation, Australia.

Lucas, P.H.C. (1992). *Protected Landscapes: A guide for policy-makers and planners.* Chapman and Hall, London, UK.

MacKinnon, J., MacKinnon, K., Child, G. and Thorsell, J. (1986). *Managing Protected Areas in the Tropics.* IUCN, Gland, Switzerland and Cambridge, UK.

McCool, S.F. Planning for Tourism in National Parks and Protected Areas: principles and concepts. In *Tourism in National Parks and Protected Areas* (in prep.).

Melamari, L (1993). Planning for Development in National Parks. Paper presented at the Wildlife Division Annual Meeting, Tanzania 1993 (unpublished).

National Parks and Wildlife Service, New South Wales (1985). Internal memos on the subject of Plans for Management (unpublished).

National Trust for England, Wales and N.Ireland (1995). *Linking People and Place.* The National Trust, Cirencester, UK.

National Trust for Scotland (2000). Management planning Manual (working draft). Unpublished.

Ndosi, O.M. (1992). Preparing Management Plans for Protected Areas. In W.J. Lusigi. *Management Protected Areas in Africa: report from a workshop on protected area management in Africa, Mweka, Tanzania.* Pp.117–124.

Noss, R. (1995). *Maintaining Ecological Integrity in Representative Reserve Networks.* WWF Canada/WWF USA Discussion Paper.

Ortega-Rubia, A. and Arguelles-Mendez, C. (1999). Management Plans for Natural Protected Areas in Mexico: La Sierra de la Laguna Case Study. *International Journal of Sustainable Development and World Ecology* **6**:68–75.

Parks Canada (1978). *Planning Process for National Parks.* Parks Canada, Ottawa, Canada.

Parr, J. (1998). Discussion paper for Protected Area Managers Writing a Management Plan. *Tiger Paper* **25(2)**:9–13.

Phillips, A. (2002). *Management Guidelines for IUCN Category V Protected Areas Protected Landscapes/seascapes.* IUCN, Gland, Switzerland, and Cambridge, UK.

Phillips, A. [in print] *Turning Ideas on their Head: The New Paradigm for Protected Areas.* Conservation Study Institute paper, CSI, Woodstock, VT, USA.

Prosser, L. (1977). A model for Planning and Managing National Parks. Ph.D. thesis, Ballarat College of Advanced Education (unpublished).

Ramsar Convention Bureau, 2000. *Ramsar handbooks for the wise use of wetlands.* Gland, Switzerland.

Ritter, D. (1997). Limits of Acceptable Change Planning in the Selway-Bitterroot Wilderness 1985–97. In *Proceedings – Limits of Acceptable Change and Related Planning Processes: progress and future directions.* US Dept of Agriculture Forest Service. General Technical Report.

Rogers, K. (1998). Managing Science/Management Partnerships: A challenge of Adaptive Management. *Conservation Ecology* [online] **2(2)** R1. www.consecol.org/vol2/iss2/resp1.

Rogers, K. and Bestbier, R. (1997). *Development of a Protocol for the Definition of the Desired State of Riverine Systems of South Africa.* South African Wetlands Conservation Programme, Department of Environmental Affairs and Tourism, Pretoria, South Africa.

Rogers, K., Roux, D. and Biggs, H. (2000). Challenges for Catchment Management Agencies: lessons from bureaucracies, business and resource management. *Water SA* **26(4)**:505–11. Available on line www.wrc.org.za.

RSPB (1999). *Management Plan Guidance Notes, Version 5.* RSPB, Sandy, UK.

Salaksy, N., Margoluis, R. and Redford, K. (2001). *Adaptive Management: a tool for conservation practitioners.* Biodiversity Support Program/WWF-US. Available online www.BSPonline.org.

Salm, R.V. and Clark, J.R. (1989). *Marine and Coastal Protected Areas: a guide for planners and managers.* IUCN, Gland, Switzerland and Cambridge, UK.

Sandwith, T.S. (1997). *Protected Area Management Plan Format.* Natal Parks Board, Pietermaritzburg, South Africa.

Sandwith, T., Shine, C., Hamilton, L. and Sheppard, D. (2001). *Transboundary Protected Areas for Peace and Cooperation.* IUCN, Gland, Switzerland and Cambridge, UK.

Scholte, P. (2000). Towards Consensual Park Management Planning in Africa. Opinion in *Oryx* **34(2)**:87–9.

South African National Parks (1997). *Management Plan for Kruger National Park. Volume VII: An objectives hierarchy for the management of Kruger National Park.* Available online www.parks-sa.co.za.

Thorsell, J. (1995) A Practical Approach to the Preparation of Management Plans for Natural Heritage Sites. Background paper prepared for Arab Region Training Course, Egypt 1995 (unpublished).

US National Parks Service (1998). *Director's Order #2: Park Planning.* Available online www.nps.gov/refdesk/Dorders/Dorder2.html.

Vollbon, T. (no date). Management Planning – present and future trends. Queensland National Parks Service (unpublished).

Wild, R.G. and Mutebi, J. (1997). Bwindi Impenetrable Forest, Uganda: Conservation through Collaborative Management. *Nature and Resources* **33**:3–4, UNESCO.

Wood, J.B. and Warren, A. (1978). A Handbook for the Preparation of Management Plans. University College London, Discussion Papers in Conservation, No. 18.

Young, E.B. (1992). Tanzania National Parks Management Planning project. Strategic Planning Process Kilimanjaro National Park. Paper Presented at the IVth World Congress on National Parks, Caracas. 1992 (unpublished).

Young, C. and Young, B. (1993). *Park Planning: A training manual (Instructors Guide).* College of African Wildlife Management, Mweka, Tanzania.